Praise for Lea

"*Leading with a Lens of Inquiry* will stretch readers to consider how to look at leading in a new way. Instead of undertaking the actions of a 'task and tell' manager, Vance encourages leaders to adopt an inquiry mindset that encourages teachers to be more curious around their practice and become an even more reflective practitioner. She provides questions to consider, strategies to use, and resources to support readers to take this mindset into their meetings, discussions, and professional learning opportunities. Education needs this inquiry mindset, and Vance helps us make it a more common way of thinking in our schools."

—**Jennifer Abrams**, communications consultant and author of *Having Hard Conversations*

"Vance's book offers a sensible and indispensable guide for leading inquiry-based schools. No matter your role in the school community, *Leading with a Lens of Inquiry* offers just the right mix of thoughtful prose, personal stories, reflective questions, and creative structures. What a gift this book is to the global inquiry community."

—**Kimberly Mitchell**, educator and author of *Experience Inquiry*

"If we want curiosity in the classroom and for agency and exploration to shape the student experience, the ways in which schools are led cannot be overlooked as a catalyst for these conditions. Vance hits the mark on how inquiry communities are cultivated, how they are nurtured, and how they thrive. Her gentle and knowledgeable guidance provides readers with a direct lens into how the values of constructivism take root. As I have experienced on many occasions, Vance has a way with words that invites you in and takes care of you. A coach at heart and an inquirer in practice, her work is sure to leave a magical mark on you."

—**Trevor MacKenzie**, educator and author of *Dive into Inquiry* and *Inquiry Mindset* series

"*Leading with a Lens of Inquiry* inspires and guides leaders to transform their daily work from drudgery to joyful, creative, and reflective inquiry. By shifting their frame of reference from leadership as a directive practice to leadership as an inquiry process, Vance encourages leaders to apply the principles of constructivism, creativity, and collaboration in their role as lead learners within their schools and school systems. Using authentic examples and strategies from her own leadership journey, Vance invites readers to investigate how curiosity, questioning, and listening serve as core skills to engage colleagues and staff in continuous exploration. The inquiry lens holds potential to inspire educator and student learning."

—**Joellen Killion**, senior advisor at Learning Forward

"This book makes me both very glad and also sad. I'm glad that educational leaders and teachers have this very rich, experience-proved set of practices to use inquiry as a major leadership practice. Especially at this time of chaos and uncertainty, sane leaders know to engage people fully and to rely on their creativity, generosity, and motivation to contribute, even as things keep changing. This book is a great source for these practices. What saddens me is that after all these years, we still have to convince leaders to create the conditions for people to develop and use our essential human capacities of curiosity, creativity, learning, and community. We should have learned this decades ago, and now our very future depends on it."

—**Margaret J. Wheatley, EdD**, author of nine books, including *Leadership and the New Science* and *Who Do We Choose To Be*

"At a moment when answers to our biggest challenges are so hard to come by, it's imperative that educators develop dispositions of inquiry in their classrooms and in their own lives. *Leading with a Lens of Inquiry* provides a great framework for centering questions to cultivate curiosity, innovation, and much-needed change in our work with students and in our school communities. It's a roadmap for developing the crucial ability to learn our way through what is by all accounts a fast-changing and increasingly complex present and future."

—**Will Richardson**, education thought leader, speaker, and author

"*Leading with a Lens of Inquiry* arrives at a time when leaders are looking for ways to support, grow, and engage their staff. Through shared personal experiences, storytelling, and excellent visuals, Jessica guides us through inquiry as a practice that can be fun, curious, and full of connections for our educators and therefore their students. The act of leading with a lens of inquiry can be uncomfortable, but Vance finds a way to make it attainable for every leader through an invitation to practice in many different and fun ways.

"I especially appreciate the intention around cultivating a reflective practice because, as she says, 'reflection lies at the heart of all inquiry learning.' She models this throughout the book with pause-and-reflect guiding questions that enable you to practice and engage with your learning. This book is the path forward for leaders who want to create that shift toward inquiry throughout their classrooms and school culture! I will definitely be adding this book to my list of must-reads for leaders in the world of education."

—**Lisa Baylis, MEd**, educator, speaker, and author of *Self-Compassion for Educators*

"*Leading with a Lens of Inquiry* speaks my language. This is a fresh and thoughtful approach to leadership and coaching, written in a warm and approachable style. Packed full of practical examples and incisive reflection questions, this book is such a valuable resource for anyone looking to rethink their approach to leadership. The values and ideas that are embodied here resonate deeply with my own work with visual and art inquiry; I loved the six characteristics for developing a reflective practice, the use of thinking routines for 'slow listening,' and the careful attention paid to curiosity and questioning."

—**Claire Bown**, founder of Thinking Museum

"It's time to rethink the whole concept of leadership—in the larger world as well as in the education world. *Leading with a Lens of Inquiry* is an excellent primer on how to lead with curiosity, open-mindedness, listening, and lots (and lots) of questions. How might we become inquiry leaders? Start by reading this book."

—**Warren Berger**, author of *A More Beautiful Question*

"True inquiry requires awareness of self and our surroundings, and awareness requires pause. *Leading with a Lens of Inquiry* is a gentle invitation to reflect over our own teaching practice, and to explore the possibilities of an inquiry-based approach on teaching and learning through leadership. Vance's passion for inquiry is obvious, and she has a gift for asking questions—using the type of questioning that can spark further inquiry. I love the way Jessica's book invites us to pause and reflect before moving on to the next lessons, in the same way we might invite our students to pause and reflect over their own learning. As she tells us, inquiry can be messy and uncomfortable but also beautiful. You can't help but feel inspired and motivated to dive headfirst into the wonderful world of inquiry while reading this book."

—**Karen Myrick**, IB/PYP educator, certified mindfulness instructor MBSR, Mindfulness in Schools

"Jessica Vance's book, *Leading with a Lens of Inquiry*, is a powerful and change-making tool for leaders. It is a must-have on your bookshelf as your school, district, and system continue to propel forward toward an inquiry approach that fully supports, responds to, and honors the whole child. Full of practical and intentional steps, Vance will support you as you shift toward a shared leadership approach that builds off the interests, strengths, and questions of your educators, all while nourishing and responding to your student community. The ripple effect of leading educators with an inquiry mindset will powerfully support everyone in your learning community."

—**Rebecca Bushby** (Bathurst-Hunt), educator and author

"*Leading with a Lens of Inquiry* takes a powerful stance: Teachers deserve to learn just as much as their students. Each chapter draws a parallel between inquiry-based learning in the classroom to discuss practical ways to build a culture of curiosity, creativity, and joy for the adults in schools. Jessica's personal anecdotes and questions throughout the book feel like sitting down with a trusted thought partner to unpack the often nebulous concept of leadership."

—**Natalie Vardabasso**, assessment specialist and consultant

"*Leading with a Lens of Inquiry* is a well-crafted resource for school leaders who are looking to support a culture of inquiry in their schools. Vance does a brilliant job of exploring the challenges associated with building a culture of inquiry while also offering practical solutions. She references her own teaching and learning experiences to reinforce the importance of focussing on the way in which we learn. She highlights the parallels between student learners and adult learners and provides the reader with coaching and leading strategies to maximize inquiry learning opportunities. She clearly identifies the value of questioning, while acknowledging that it is a learned skill which requires support and practice. I would recommend this book for anyone who is interested in building an inquiry-driven learning culture."

—**James Nottingham**, founder and CEO of ChallengingLearning.com

"This is a book that not only talks about the importance of leading with inquiry but it also provides a reading and learning experience that actively encourages inquiry and reflection throughout. In other words, this is a book that walks the walk. There are very big ideas here about learning and professional growth that are translated into actionable steps that can be implemented. What could be better than that for creating invaluable professional learning opportunities?"

—**Dan Rothstein**, co-director of Democracy-Building Program at the Right Question Institute; co-author of *Make Just One Change*

Leading with a Lens of Inquiry

Cultivating Conditions for Curiosity and Empowering Agency

Jessica Vance

Leading with a Lens of Inquiry
© 2022 by Jessica Vance

All rights reserved. No part of this publication may be reproduced in any form or by any electronic or mechanical means, including information storage and retrieval systems, without permission in writing by the publisher, except by a reviewer who may quote brief passages in a review. For information regarding permission, contact the publisher at elevatebooksedu.com.

> These books are available at special discounts when purchased in quantity for use as premiums, promotions, fundraising and educational use. For inquiries and details, contact the publisher at elevatebooksedu.com.

Editing and Layout by My Writers' Connection

Published by Elevate Books EDU
Library of Congress Control Number: 2022936723
Paperback ISBN: 979-8-9851374-3-9
eBook ISBN: 979-8-9851374-4-6

*This book is dedicated to my two little leaders,
Sawyer and Londyn.*

Contents

Foreword by Kath Murdoch xiii
Roots of Wonderings xix

Chapter 1: Inquiry as a Framework for Leadership 1
Chapter 2: Cultivating a Reflective Practice 17
Chapter 3: Dispositions of an Inquiry Leader 37
Chapter 4: The Ripple Effect 57
Chapter 5: Leading Is Listening 81
Chapter 6: Making the Learning Visible 101
Chapter 7: Nurturing a Culture of Inquiry 117
Concluding with a Call to Action 137

Suggested Reading 145
Bibliography 149
Acknowledgments 151
About the Author 153
About the Illustrator 154

Foreword

The culture of a classroom is palpable. It is communicated through the arrangement of furniture, what is on the walls, the words used (and not used) by educators and learners, the movement of people, the presence of laughter, the tone of discourse, and the ease with which one is welcomed into the space. This culture, often obvious within minutes of entering, is, of course, largely determined by the educators themselves. As Haim Ginott famously reminded us, it is the teacher who is the decisive element in the classroom and the teacher whose personal approach "creates the climate."

For over thirty years, I have had the privilege of visiting countless classrooms throughout the world and have experienced what can be quite stark differences between the learning climates in each. But entering a classroom begins with entering a school. And just as the classroom climate is so strongly determined by the teacher, leaders of schools hold similar power and the culture *they* create is equally palpable. The values and dispositions of leaders fuel their language and their actions, which, in turn, create culture. That culture can either stimulate or stifle the initiative, motivation, agency, and joy experienced by educators in the community which of course flows on to their interactions with students. In my work as a consultant in inquiry-based learning, I have seen over and over again the powerful impact leaders can have in creating cultures within which *inquiry* thrives for both students and teachers. As an outsider stepping into schools on a regular basis to support their inquiry journeys, I can say unequivocally that the success of my work ultimately depends on the way it is led on the *inside*. Inquiry learning in classrooms thrives when leaders—team leaders, curriculum leaders, coordinators, principals, and their deputies—bring an inquiry stance to *their* work with colleagues, and when the school itself is reimagined as what Riordan and Caillier (2018) describe as an "equitable community of inquiry." They argue that

> The diversity of our students, the complexity of the world, and the urgency of our current condition demand a paradigm shift where schools, rather than purveyors of inert knowledge, serve as centers of community inquiry and action.

The literature on educational leadership has a long and deep history. It is no exaggeration to describe the field as a vast and complex one and the role of leaders in schools as relentlessly demanding—never more so than during the last two years of a worldwide pandemic. The intensification of the work of school leaders should not be underestimated. Pressures at system level can be overwhelming, leaving contemporary leaders with the unenviable task of managing competing forces of accountability, administration, and the day-to-day work required to support diverse communities of teachers, young learners, and their families.

So it is with gratitude and optimism that I read this beautiful offering from Jessica Vance, who warmly invites leaders to position themselves, first and foremost, as inquirers. In *Leading with a Lens of Inquiry*, Jessica shares her personal journey of discovering new approaches to leadership with a highly engaging, accessible writing style and a pace that gently provokes curiosity and routinely nudges the reader to adopt an intentional, reflective stance.

Both school leadership *and* professional learning can suffer from a perceived hypocrisy that leaves teachers cynical and mistrustful. It is easy for those in positions of power to talk about the importance of inquiry-based values such as curiosity, agency, equity, collaboration, co-construction, and learners at the center but this rhetoric is not always matched by action. Indeed, it is not uncommon to hear inquiry-based practices championed for the classroom in contexts that maintain traditional, didactic approaches to leadership and teacher learning. This familiar tension is addressed early on in Vance's book and becomes, in many ways, the rationale for what follows:

> *I could clearly see the disconnectedness between our messaging about what was best for student learning and how we delivered that message to teachers.*

Rather than ignoring this glaring contradiction, Jessica enthusiastically tackles the challenge of aligning her approach to leadership with the ways she has worked as an inquiry-based classroom teacher. It's not enough to espouse the values underpinning inquiry in a school; leaders need to BE inquirers and have the same commitment to an open, collaborative community of learners we endeavor to nurture as we teach. Like the inquiry approach itself, leading as an act of inquiry can suffer from a misinterpretation of it as a warm and fuzzy, *laissez-faire* style. I have been fortunate to work with some of the most inquiry-oriented, effective leaders in schools around the world, and there could be nothing further from the truth. These leaders are strategic, organized, decisive, and highly intentional in all they do. They bring empathy and compassion to their work, but this does not mean they abandon high expectations and a vigorous commitment to improvement. Leading with a lens of inquiry requires deep engagement and a willingness to pursue continuous learning.

Central to inquiry-based leadership is the way in which leaders see themselves and think about their role—indeed, their *dispositions* or mindsets drive their actions. The leadership dispositions Jessica articulates, drawn from her lived experience as a practitioner, strongly echo much of what scholars such as Kaser and Halbert (2009) and Lieberman and Miller (2005) and others have researched and championed for many years. It is the mindsets of leaders to which we must draw our attention, and the combination of what Kaser and Halbert describe as "genuine inquiry mindedness" with intense moral purpose has the potential to create the highly effective and equitable learning environments for which we strive.

While inquiry-based leadership begins with values and dispositions or mindsets, it also requires (just as in the classroom) a rich repertoire of strategies and techniques to help engage, support, coach, question, and collaborate with colleagues. Drawing on the work of a range of experts in the field of inquiry and visible thinking, Jessica provides authentic and very helpful examples of the use of visible thinking routines, questioning techniques, ideas for documentation, and a pleasingly nuanced use of my own inquiry cycle, recognizing that just as the cycle is neither rigid nor sequential in the classroom, neither is it when applied to teacher inquiry. The explanations of these processes and examples of her successful use of them with colleagues is an invaluable offering—particularly to teachers new to leadership, who will be reassured that the essence of inquiry-based practice holds true regardless of whether they are working with children or adults. Coupled with these practical examples, this text is filled with beautiful questions that invite leaders to contemplate the way they work. These are questions entire schools can use to re-examine the kind of learning community they want to be. Jessica's examples, together with the challenges and recommendations she shares, are simple, strongly relatable, and accessible, making this an ideal text for leaders new to their role or those wishing to reflect and refresh their thinking.

Around the world, there is a growing discontent with leadership paradigms rooted in inequity, fueled by individualism, and harnessed to a relationship with the planet that is no longer sustainable. As I write, a national election in my own country looms, with a heightened degree of despair and anger amongst young people that is hard to ignore. More people are standing as independent candidates, challenging what feels like a leadership approach past its use-by date—with many arguing the time has come to truly listen to the community and to listen to the planet. Our deeply troubled times cry out for courageous, agile leaders prepared to stay relentlessly curious, to listen, to collaborate, to be comfortable with nuance and complexity, and to remain what Adam Grant describes as "confidently humble." Leaders in schools around the world have the opportunity—indeed the responsibility—to demonstrate to our young people real alternatives to the rigid, simplistic, authoritarian, top-down models of the past.

The late, great Ken Robinson often used the analogy of a garden when he described the work of teachers. He reminded us that no teacher can make a student learn but what they can do is to create the right conditions for those learners to grow. In the same way, Jessica reminds us that the role of the leader is to create the conditions for a flourishing garden—one that is interconnected, diverse in nature, and teeming with robust life. Leaders cannot make teachers work in inquiry-based ways, but they can indeed create the conditions that help inquiry flourish throughout a school. This book is a welcome addition to the toolkit for school leaders in contemporary school settings. In Jessica's words, it is just what you need to "get *in* the learning."

In Part 4, Jessica offers her readers the metaphor of the stone thrown into the pond to describe the ripple effect that leading with an inquiry lens can have. The book you are holding in your hands has the potential to be a "stone" in itself. Perhaps you are an aspiring leader, and the questions Jessica raises for you will influence the way you approach your new role. Perhaps you already lead with an inquiry lens and are considering how you might pass this book to a young teacher in whom you see potential for this kind of work. Regardless of where you are in your journey, may you heed Jessica's call to action by taking that next step with an even stronger resolve to lead with courage, curiosity, and the kind of playfulness that cultivates curiosity and courage in those around you.

Our teachers, children, and their families deserve nothing less.

—Kath Murdoch
teacher, consultant, and author of *Getting Personal with Inquiry Learning*

Roots of Wonderings

Julie and I (Jessica) *accidentally* shared an office. I say "accidentally" because, as happens when schools are at capacity, classrooms—as well as the shared office spaces for the instructional support staff, such as coaches, coordinators, technology specialists, and curriculum coordinators—get shuffled and reshuffled. During a year of personal and professional change, I found myself at a new school in a new leadership position. Making space for everyone required shuffling, and what seemed like an insignificant office assignment led to something greater than either of us could have ever imagined.

Our accidental beginning uncovered the approach to leadership you will read about in this book. What started as two colleagues sharing four walls turned into an inquiry into *our* roles as leaders. We carefully observed each other as we interacted with the teachers we supported. We asked big questions about the systems we were part of, and we ultimately built a trusting relationship that allowed us to continually push each other to grow along the way.

> Our body of work exists because of the tireless efforts of other inquiry leaders who have come before us. Judy Halbert and Linda Kaser's committed work lay some of the foundation for leading with an inquiry mindset in our systems and schools. Take a deeper look at their book *The Spiral Playbook* as you continue to find out more about tangible actions and mindsets we take as leaders.

It's worth noting here that the same leaders at the helm during that time of transition continue to lead us today. Without their trust, questions, and the space they provided that allowed us to explore our leadership roles, we wouldn't have the stories shared with you in this book. We, too, needed leaders who stepped back so we could step forward. These brave inquiry-minded administrators were committed to developing our capacities as leaders and remained curious about how we were facilitating adult learning on our campus. It was through our work together, with our teachers and with our leaders, that we discovered what we valued and ultimately redefined what leadership meant to us.

After more than a decade as a classroom teacher, I moved into the role of program coordinator. I'd watch Julie, our technology coordinator, interact with teachers who came into our office to notify her of a computer problem or to ask which new app might be best to offer students who were trying to complete their end-of-unit projects. Instead of telling them the answer or jumping up quickly to fix the problem herself, she would always reply with a question. I was curious: *Why didn't Julie immediately give our colleagues what they were seeking?*

Facing her question, the teachers furrowed their brows or grimaced in frustration. They came to her in search of an answer, not another question! As Julie leaned toward them with an inquisitive look, however, there was a quick softening to the teacher's body language and tone of voice, followed by a deep sigh as they unpacked the technology issue they were facing. They shared what they had tried, and Julie would again use a simple, open-ended question to support the teachers' thought processes, allowing them the space to make connections based on their previous experiences. Invariably, she would gently nudge the teacher's thinking with questions that often started with, "I wonder . . ." or "What do you think about . . . ?"

Julie would encourage the teachers with a few strategies to try and a promise to circle back with them a bit later. Even when they were still a bit unsure, the teachers left our office with smiles on their faces, ready to tackle their issues with a bit more confidence.

As we got to know each other better, I learned that she would later visit the teachers' classrooms and offer to teach alongside them, work with students in small groups, and offer connection ideas for upcoming learning experiences as they pursued their technology integration journey. After class, she took time to ask the teachers how they thought it went and found ways to celebrate their successes, which further encouraged their desire for innovation.

Seeing these exchanges reminded me of the interactions I'd had with students in my own inquiry classroom. I would, more often than not, use student questions to guide much of the learning or use a variety of tools and graphic organizers, which allowed my learners and me to collect data in the form of student feedback and experiences. I had regularly asked my students about systems in the classroom or to reflect on their feelings about the concepts we would be exploring together in a particular subject area. Later, I would analyze this data with the students. We would use calendars to map out an upcoming writing unit, create backward-planned learning experiences based on their inquiries, and mark checkpoints along the way to ensure understanding and progress on our projects. Sometimes the data would lead us to reorganize the time we spent working and learning together. Students would help me brainstorm the different ways they could learn, including activities they recognized that helped them practice particular skills and even the ways I could best support them while they were working independently.

The more I asked my students questions, the more they told me. The more they talked, the more I listened. And the more I listened, the more I noticed the shifts in my classroom, in my practice, and in my students. Seeing Julie's approach to supporting adult learning aligned with what I knew about supporting student learning. I could see the inquiry approach in her coaching and leadership, something I valued in my own classroom, and it made me wonder:

- Were the ways I built relationships and trust with my students applicable to my current position in supporting adult learners, teachers, and colleagues?
- What values did I hold as a classroom teacher that allowed me to trust my students enough to guide the learning? What values do I hold now as a leader?
- How could questions be used to support the adult learners on my campus?
- Where was there space to let go and allow the teachers to help design the learning we would unpack together during team meetings or after-school professional development sessions?
- What was my purpose as a campus leader? What defines an impactful leader? And in what ways were our roles as leaders similar to those of a teacher working with students?

As Julie and I continued working alongside each other, we brought these questions to our roles as both leaders and learners. These questions catapulted countless conversations in our office, led to our own research about the ways that people learn best and make meaning for themselves, and helped us continually reflect on our purpose and value as leaders. We came back to these questions as we led book studies to help support learning across the campus, visited classrooms to celebrate student learning, made outlines for our professional development plans for the school year, and coached teachers as they worked toward their personal goals.

Our work with and for teachers elevated two particular questions that became the foundation for our approach as educators:

What do you value?

and

Who is a leader?

These questions are big. They take time to digest, and only through personal experience and quiet reflection can one begin to truly unpack them. Our values are evidenced to others through our actions. They are shaped through the challenges we face, the people in our lives, the milestones, the celebrations, and, of course, the failures. Our work together over the next five years continued to add more layers of meaning and a deeper understanding to these questions. What stood out to us was evident:

We valued the connections and relationships that came with our roles.

We valued the agency of our learners (the teachers) and the action they took as they reflected on their practice.

We valued listening.

We valued the *process* of learning—which at times is unpredictable. This value allowed us to co-construct meaning and further stretch ourselves in our leadership roles.

We valued the feedback from our learners and how our leadership and soft guidance impacted the way teachers taught and, in turn, how learners learned.

The journey and unexpected nature of where we began may seem so insignificant, even happenstance; however, this subtlety is what differentiates an inquiry approach to teaching and learning from a more traditional approach to the practice. Leading with a lens of inquiry inspires others to approach teaching with a lens of inquiry. Simply put, if we want inquiry for our kids, adults need it too.

Leading with a Lens of Inquiry is about rethinking our approach to the adult learners in our buildings. It's about having fun. It's about asking questions. It's about considering the value of a shared leadership approach that empowers our teachers to reflect and refine their teaching practice continually. It's about responding to the needs, learning styles, and interests of those we lead, just as teachers in the classroom respond to their students.

This book reveals the leader's inquiry journey. I'll share the thinking and reflections that evolved as, over time, our approach to leadership shifted. I've included a series of reflective questions throughout each of the chapters and invite you to pause and reflect on your practice as a leader. As you read these questions you may at times find yourself inspired, making immediate connections to the reading and to your own practice as a leader. At other times, you may find yourself needing to sit with these questions a bit longer, referring to them at a later date, or perhaps bringing them to a trusted colleague or leadership team for further discussion. I urge you to share your thinking, questions, and ideas with your professional learning network (PLN). Adding to the collective conversation of #leadingwithinquiry helps us all refine our practice. However you decide to do so, I ask that you lean into these questions. Look at them as opportunities to build your capacities as a reflective leader and learner.

In keeping with the theme of this work, let's pause here to reflect. Jot down an intention you have before continuing. What do you hope to gain from this book? Perhaps an intention seems too big, too bold at this time. How would you like to feel after your reading this week? What word or phrase first comes to mind?

> Want to deepen your understanding of intentions and the nuanced differences between intentions and goals? Listen to this *Optimal Living Daily* podcast episode by Stephen Warley titled "Stop Making Goals; Set Intentions Instead." It's only twelve minutes long. I am sure it will resonate with you.

As you settle into an idea or word, I'll share my intention with you.

My intentions are to inspire you to lead with an inquiry approach and to offer you tools that will support you in the process so you can, in turn, empower those around you.

Through the experiences shared, I hope you connect and find value in a way that is meaningful for you. I encourage you to return to this space, checking in with your intention and observing how it shifts throughout your reading. This is *your* learning experience.

Now, let's get started, shall we?

Chapter 1
Inquiry as a Framework for Leadership

Inquiry learning is about making connections. As learners, we all have experiences from which we draw when facing new challenges. An inquiry-based approach is a process by which a learner uses their background knowledge as they approach new situations and asks questions to find out more, uncovering, in turn, new layers of understanding about the world around them. A teacher's role in this process is one of facilitator, artfully guiding the learning, pushing students in ways that both challenge and support their learning styles and needs. Inquiry is an approach to teaching and learning that honors the learner, highlighting the process of learning over time through rich and meaningful interactions between the teacher and student. Those who teach with this lens guide the learning in their classrooms with significant, relevant, engaging, and challenging learning experiences. They see the benefits of this practice impacting their learners, supporting them in not only their development of skills across the subject areas but also in their dispositions as learners, developing skills such as communication, thinking, and questioning that will serve them no matter where their learning takes them.

Knowing that the benefits of an inquiry practice impact *all* students, empowering children to develop into confident, independent learners, the public school where I served as a program coordinator held the framework of inquiry close to the heart of all programming on our campus. We focused much of our time on supporting teachers as they planned lessons with this inquiry lens—coaching our new teachers as they stepped into their own classrooms for the first time and encouraging our returning teachers, who valued the process of continuous improvement. Time and time again, we would guide our teachers back to the structure of inquiry, sorting through ideas during collaborative team planning meetings and supporting them as they made sense of new resources and planned new learning opportunities for their students to explore. Repeatedly, however, we observed a disconnection between messaging at the school level and expectations at the district level. There was a clear tension between what we were cultivating as an inquiry school and the outside forces that teachers felt pulled toward. We wondered:

- What was causing our teachers to revert to more complacent and teacher-centric ways of teaching?
- Why did they need constant nudging and reminding of the benefits of an inquiry-based approach?
- Were they simply going back to what was comfortable out of habit?

Our teachers had witnessed the benefits of an inquiry approach with their learners in their classrooms. We heard them share countless stories about the powerful learning experiences that resulted in students taking action by building their own websites to promote their canned-food drives or community clean-up events. We saw students who developed skills that enabled them to reflect as learners and set personal goals for themselves. We received endless parent feedback that, although this approach to teaching and learning was different from what they had experienced as a student, they could see how their children owned their role in the process of learning and were excited about school in a way they (the parents) had not experienced as young scholars.

Again, we wondered: With the clear benefits right in front of us all, why were we continually having to reframe and refocus teachers' attention and ways of thinking?

As former classroom teachers ourselves, we paused and put ourselves (mentally) back into the classroom in an attempt to make sense of the conflicting evidence. We evaluated all angles of the issues and asked even more questions:

- Was our guidance and approach to support really meeting our teachers where they were?
- What was the underlying cause that continued to drive the issues we were facing?

Reflection Leads to Insights

Recalling my early classroom teaching experiences, I remembered that implementing an inquiry approach felt similar to that of learning a new language—a new language of teaching that I had not practiced during my time as a student teacher or throughout my preparatory coursework. I felt confused by what the administration and instructional coaches on my campus meant when they said that I should be facilitating the learning process and didn't feel confident that my students would know what we needed to cover during the school year.

During the first few years of my career, I engaged in an *unlearning* of everything that *I thought that I knew* as a teacher. In the school setting, I faced an approach to learning that was different from what I had experienced as a young student and later in the courses that I took in college. State standards and district expectations clearly identified the *what* that was required of me and my teaching. But I saw that I had control over *how* I would guide my students to meet those standards and expectations.

By pulling apart state standards and collaborating with my colleagues, I carefully designed learning experiences that invited connection, curiosity, and personal meaning for all students. The standards would remain my goal for students, but they would not be my defining mark of where the learning stopped and started.

I tested the questions I would use to guide the lessons. I experimented with different graphic organizers, tools, and other similar structures to get feedback from my students. I infused my personal reflection at the end of each day to determine next steps in learning. Through this unlearning process, I became familiar with "backward design" in my unit planning and slowly learned to trust my students.

My questions became a launchpad for learning. I viewed them as an invitation for exploration into the concepts and topics in the units that I was planning. I then modeled my thinking and questions for my students, highlighting my role as a continuous learner. Taking part in the inquiry process myself allowed me to become increasingly more comfortable with talking less so my students could talk more and own their roles as learners in my classroom.

Each of these shifts in my practice expanded my understanding of and vision for my role as an educator and how I could best serve my students in the process of learning. I saw that the more I let go while remaining purposeful, the more empowered my students became. They knew I trusted them as learners and would be listening to them and using their feedback to guide our next steps *together*.

When, as a program coordinator, I reflected on my experience in the classroom and my process of learning and unlearning, I was able to better understand why the shift to inquiry seemed so difficult for our teachers.

We do what we are taught. What we see modeled reinforces our teaching practice.

I had always worked and collaborated with strong mentor teachers who shared different strategies and lessons with me. I regularly sought out support and resources from instructional coaches on my campus.

Not one of those mentors or leaders, however, guided my professional learning with the framework of inquiry. I wonder how my practice might have evolved had my mentors and teachers come alongside me in my new learning with an inquiry frame of mind. Without my own observations and reflections, it would have been easy to revert to traditional approaches to teaching and learning. Those approaches were what I knew; they were comfortable. But I knew I wanted something more, for both myself and my students.

I had witnessed a powerful shift in learning using inquiry with students in the classroom. My experience begged the question: What type of learning was possible if leaders coached and guided their staff with an inquiry mindset?

A Shift toward Modeling Inquiry

In the role of a campus leader, I participated in weekly grade-level meetings, facilitated professional development after school, and supported both seasoned and new teachers. Upon reflection, I could clearly see the disconnectedness between our messaging about what was best for student learning and how we delivered that message to teachers. We were talking instead of listening and telling instead of exploring together. We let the systems rule our training approach instead of viewing those systems as a frame within which we could design impactful experiences for our learners: the teachers we supported. No wonder we had all become frustrated with the monotonous conversations about why inquiry learning wasn't possible in the classroom. Our teachers were *hearing* that inquiry worked with learners, but because they weren't *seeing* inquiry modeled, their practice didn't change.

Identifying this gap in the way we were leading the professional learning and growth of our teachers and what we were asking them to implement shifted our mindset as leaders and brought important questions to light:

- If inquiry teaching and learning was something we valued in the classroom because of the impact it had on student learning,

then why wouldn't we facilitate adult learning in our building in that same way?
- What possibilities in learning were we missing because of our narrow approach to leadership?
- How could we step back and allow our teachers to step forward?
- How could we guide our adult learners with questions and provoke their thinking as they construct their own meaning in their professional growth as educators?

We aimed to redefine our approach to leading the learning on campus by creating more space for our teachers to guide our next steps and honoring their processes as learners. As the state standards had done for me when I was a classroom teacher, our campus goals would provide the *what* behind our work together. *How* we accomplish those goals would be completely up to us as a collaborative community of learners. We, as leaders, are determined to communicate our goals and their roles as educators explicitly. We resolved to step back, slow down, and notice more, rethinking our use of time spent together. Utilizing the power of reflection throughout the inquiry process to intentionally plan our next steps, we would trust them as learners the same way we were encouraging them to trust their students in their classrooms. We would *all* be learning and leading with an inquiry mindset.

Our plans sounded great, in theory. But I'll be the first to admit that leading with a lens of inquiry requires practice and patience.

Beautiful, Messy Inquiry

Leading with a lens of inquiry can be uncomfortable. At times, the weight of leadership can feel heavy. There are parents to please, programs to oversee, and teachers and other staff to manage on a daily basis. So *how can we shift our thinking and open ourselves up to the infinite possibilities that inquiry brings to our schools while balancing the*

demands of leadership? How can we stay curious? And where can we, as leaders, begin to let go, trusting our learners a bit more in the process?

Leading with the framework of inquiry is not a free-for-all. Leading with inquiry means we value our adult learners; we lean in, listen more, and talk less. Modeling inquiry, we provide scaffolded structures to support growth and provide our teachers with the tools they need to monitor their professional development as they build both their capacity and the impact they can have on the learners in their classrooms. This inquiry mindset means we stay curious ourselves, remain open to the ways we can be better leaders, and practice this disposition as we coach. It requires that we engage in reflective conversations, showing confidence while being vulnerable enough to share our stories and admit we don't have all of the answers.

Throughout this book, I will share stories and examples of how we implemented our inquiry dreams and ideas with our adult learners. Yes, it was messy and beautiful—and worth it. Leading with a lens of inquiry has helped this powerful mindset become part of our school's practice—from the principal's office down to the youngest grade. We see its power at work in the way our learners—at all levels—take ownership, ask questions, and explore possibilities and solutions. The shift took time and intentional effort, as well as the use of tools like the inquiry cycle.

The Inquiry Cycle

The inquiry cycle illustrated below comes from the dedicated work of Kath Murdoch.[1] If you are well versed in inquiry, you may have already seen this cycle or one similar to it. It's a framework for the process of inquiry learning that helps explain the stages of the inquiry process. While its design is cyclical, learning is not. There's an ebb and flow between each of the stages, depending on our learners. Sometimes we spend more time going further with our students, listening to their passions and needs related to the ideas being explored. At other times, our students may need only a brief amount of time in the "Finding Out" stage of their learning based on pre-assessments, conversations, and thinking revealed during the "Tuning In" stage.

The cycle supports a constructivist approach to teaching and learning, a well-known pedagogical philosophy that underpins the framework of inquiry and puts the learner at the forefront. Through an active process of reflection, social interactions, and multiple learning experiences designed to encourage our learners to dig deeper into big ideas, they begin to make connections between concepts and the world around them. From there, they use those connections to solve problems and ask more questions that continue to drive the learning. Here's a quick overview of each stage:

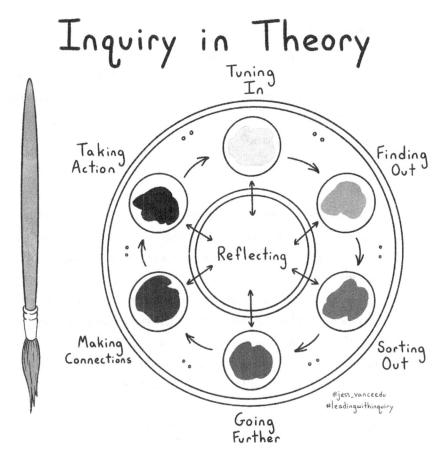

Adapted from Kath Murdoch's Inquiry Cycle

Tuning In

In this early phase of inquiry, we tune into our learners' thinking and ideas by provoking them with a series of photos or short video clips or possibly engaging in a class discussion based on some current event within our world based on a clear, big idea. Although the audiences are different, the experience and process are quite similar. We gather evidence and feedback on their initial understandings and use these as crucial data to make our next steps in the learning.

Finding Out

During this stage, we spend our time digging into new information or learning. Depending on the concept being explored, we may use direct instruction to share new information with our learners or provide them ample time to act as researchers, digging into new ideas while gathering data on their own.

Sorting

Once learners take in new information, they begin to sort through it to make sense of what they've uncovered. In the classroom, students discuss their research with a partner or share their thoughts within a small group after reading a selected piece of literature. Whether through an interview with Guy Claxton outlining the little things that teachers can do to help students build their capacities to manage and organize their own learning, an article from John Hattie on the delicate way that feedback encourages thinking, or a piece by Jay McTighe on how to check for understanding in the classroom, we provide space for our adult learners, too, to sort through resources and the rich ideas they present to us. This phase of the learning is where the learner is able to make personal meaning based on their findings, perhaps even identifying how their thinking has begun to change.

Going Further

Through personal reflection, learners and teachers (or leaders) identify together how their ideas have shifted. During this phase of the learning, the learner naturally begins to raise new questions, determining what possible next steps may be taken. Oftentimes, the learners' ideas may be challenged in this stage, requiring the teacher to extend learning through differentiated experiences to meet the learners where they are.

Making Connections

While analyzing data and drawing new conclusions are naturally present in the learning process, in this stage, learners explicitly synthesize their learning. Students may analyze their initial questions, share their learning with the community of learners, and reflect on what they may do with their new learning.

Taking Action

This stage of the inquiry cycle requires learners to reflect on how their thinking or behavior may have changed based on their inquiry experience. Learners transfer their insights by evaluating potential actions, reflecting on their experiences, and asking themselves, *What can I do now?*

Communication and **reflection** occur continuously throughout the inquiry process. Using these vital pieces to the puzzle, our learners communicate with their peers to build on their understanding of the big ideas they are exploring, challenge one another's thinking by sharing their unique perspectives, and reflect as they continue to construct and make personal meaning of the learning.

We all learn in this way, don't we? Our natural curiosities are piqued by some event or other experience, and we make connections based on what we already know about the topic, sort through this new information, and draw new conclusions. For most of us, the traditional systems and structures of school don't support the natural ways we learn. Additionally, we spend most of our life learning outside of school, and, in doing so, we find the learning styles and structures that work best for our personal needs.

Learning is not a prescriptive sequence; however, the inquiry cycle provides a framework for the facilitator to support thinking and conversation. We keep this framework on prominent display in our school. It is pinned to bulletin boards and included in meeting agendas. It's the tool we return to when designing and planning professional development, and we refer to it when we are coaching and supporting teachers in their own personal growth goals. This framework reminds us that our teachers are lifelong learners and that we, as leaders, can facilitate their learning in a meaningful and purposeful way when we keep an inquiry approach to our leadership.

Benefits of Leading with Inquiry

Throughout this book, you will read about the different ways that using this lens brought changes to our teachers, campus culture, and even ourselves as leaders. I've included my personal reflections on the process, as well as how, over time, our leadership team became comfortable stepping away from traditional ways of educational leadership and toward inquiry as we collaborated, reflected, and grew in our leadership capacities individually and as a team.

Below is a list of benefits we've experienced in our school as a result of leading with a lens of inquiry. Watch for them to show up in the stories I've included, as well as in your own school as you lead with inquiry:

Leaders and Teachers Become Partners in Learning.

- Relationships always come first.
- Passion, energy, and excitement are contagious.
- Connection to others helps people and the organization build resilience.
- Learning is co-constructed.
- Everyone has a voice, which ensures equity.
- Learning is personalized and meaningful.

Inquiry Leaders Motivate and Inspire.

- Leaders develop confidence within others.
- Mindful language empowers instead of stifles.
- Leaders experience greater impact.
- Leaders influence innovation.
- Inquiry leaders create a positive climate and culture.
- Everyone feels welcomed, respected, and appreciated.

Teachers Are Empowered.

- The community is strong and connected.
- Leadership becomes a shared approach.
- Curiosity is cultivated and sustained.
- Teachers are influenced to teach with an inquiry mindset.
- Passions, energy, and excitement build upon one another.
- Teacher voice is elevated.

What does it mean to lead with an inquiry mindset?

There is no one way to be an inquiry leader, but there are common mindsets that inquiry leaders share. As inquiry leaders work within our traditional educational systems, they maintain an awareness that they want to show up for themselves and for those they lead. They remain curious about their staff and how to support the process of learning. They gather feedback to reflect on and refine the ways they facilitate and support learning.

We'll dig deeper into the dispositions of an inquiry leader in Chapter 3, but I invite you to tune in and explore the mindset of an inquiry leader using the lists below. Make notes in the margins, check off ones you believe are your strengths, and highlight the areas you want to improve.

What it is...	What it's not...
• Being reflective	• Managerial
• Process oriented	• Task oriented
• Engaging in lifelong learning	• Telling
• Valuing feedback from staff	• Stifling growth
• Being comfortable with change and innovation	• Being fearful of mistakes
• Using questions as guidance	• Acting with a "fix it" mindset
• Having playful actions and mindset	• Right vs. wrong
• Knowing the value of the relationships	• Ignoring what feedback tells you
• Inviting the teachers into the spaces	• A checklist approach that leaves little space for reflective conversations
• Modeling curiosity	• Leading that values the ease of compliance
• Innovative	
• Trusting in your people	
• Supporting teachers through scaffolding	
• Including all	
• Enabling staff to have reflective conversations	
• Empowering teachers	
• Inspiring action	
• Modeling core competencies and dispositions for success	

In this book, I will share what took place at my school as our leadership team worked to support our teachers' inquiry process. You'll read about our shifts in thinking as leaders, the impact it has had on our school culture, and how this inquiry lens of leadership created partnerships in learning in our schools. I will be honest about the struggles you might face. You'll hear stories about the challenges and changes my co-leaders and I witnessed, and you'll hear reflections from the teachers we led through this process.

I have a hunch that our approaches to leading may be different from any other contemporary book on educational leadership, and for that, I'm glad. My hope is that you will accept the invitation to rethink and redefine the way you lead. I encourage you to reflect on your values, behaviors, and beliefs as a leader and to consider their impact on how you lead and, most importantly, the impact they have on those you lead. Above all, I hope you will be inspired to lead with an inquiry mindset.

Pause and Reflect

* Revisit the image and the breakdown of the inquiry cycle (pages 8–11). What do you already know about the inquiry cycle as it relates to learning? Where are there gaps in your knowledge and understanding?
* Review the table that highlights what it means to have an inquiry mindset (page 14). What qualities of an inquiry mindset make you pause and stretch your thinking?
* What characteristics do you already hold as an inquiry leader? How do you know this to be accurate?
* What benefits of leading with inquiry do you feel align with your leadership approach? What makes you say this?

Chapter 2
Cultivating a Reflective Practice

Our leadership team had spent the previous year collaboratively planning, focusing our conversations on the value of questioning in the classroom, both as a tool for igniting student thinking and as a way to drive instruction. Huddled together, we had spent hours at a time looking at sticky notes attached to see-think-wonder charts, reviewing student end-of-unit reflections, and poring over hours of documented conversations among teams of teachers about the role of ambiguity in the inquiry learning process.

Because we valued an inquiry-based approach to teaching and learning, we spent countless hours reflecting on the power of play and on the need to gently let go of the tight grip we (and our teachers) held on state standards. We wanted to allow space for genuine curiosity and learning to unfold, trusting that with guidance, students would always lead the learning where *they* needed it to go. We wholeheartedly believed that when student questions led the way, those questions would catapult the learning process to something richly meaningful and valuable to them and their teachers.

Little by little, we saw an ease settle into the classrooms. Teachers began trusting their students and grew more comfortable using student passions, ideas, and questions to lean into the inquiry process. That school year ended on a high. We celebrated the hard work we and our teachers had done to stretch ourselves in new, meaningful ways. Having teachers' end-of-the-year reflections in hand, we felt confident that the deep connections, thinking, and shifts would continue to grow into the next school year. We set personal goals for ourselves as leaders to round out the year, ready for the break of summer to recharge and confident we would return to the building with fresh eyes after some time away.

Fast forward to later that summer. It was July and time to prepare for the upcoming weeks when our returning and new teachers would be coming back to the building. As with any new start, excitement about the new year filled the air. Whether it be the calendar year in January or the start of school in the fall, new starts mean refreshed energies, new goals, and an unmarked year that is wide open to new experiences and full of potential.

As we sat down to begin our planning and preparation for the upcoming week, however, the energy quickly drained from the room. With district expectations for required training and our own housekeeping list of things we wanted to cover, the excitement and energy for the new year quickly dwindled. What we were left with was a checklist of things to complete that seemed absolutely uninspiring to the people who were responsible for facilitating it.

In the previous school year, we had seen a transformation in the approach to the practice of teaching across the campus. A passion for learning beyond the standards had grown, as had curiosity among the staff about varied approaches and learning experiences. Our school—leaders, teachers, and students—had developed a mindset that we were all in this together, which had allowed us to slow down and lean into the process of learning as it unfolded.

Now, overwhelmed by our uninspiring checklist, we asked ourselves some big questions:

- Where had the approach to thinking, questions, and curiosity we had focused on so intentionally last year gone?
- How could we so quickly fall back into old patterns, habits, and approaches to the start of a new year?
- How were we bringing the values that were changing our campus culture into our approach to professional development?
- How could we continue with the momentum of an inquiry-based approach to teaching and learning if we only brought those conversations to the table when we were talking about students?
- Why weren't we leading with inquiry starting with day one? *What were we waiting for?*

Reflection lies at the heart of all inquiry learning. As facilitators of inquiry-based teaching in the classroom, educators provide opportunities for students to reflect on their learning through intentional and collaborative classroom or peer discussions and through moments of quiet personal reflection done through journaling using open-ended sentence stems. Allowing space for these times of reflection is one of the most important ways educators lead with inquiry. Inquiry teachers know the value in providing time for students to make connections, build on new ideas, and even evaluate the changes in their thinking over time.

The same time and space are crucial in an inquiry leader's approach to the professional growth and learning of educators. Providing teachers with opportunities for collaborative discussions and moments for written reflection to process new ideas shared among colleagues after a training session or a visit to another classroom models the value of reflection and the significant impact this practice has on *all* learners.

It is critical for leaders to embody and exhibit the behaviors we want to see in our teachers. Serving as an example, we can build our teachers' capacity for inquiry, and, in turn, they will be better equipped to create the conditions for deep and powerful learning in their classrooms.

Understanding that reality, we knew we needed to be honest with ourselves, take a hard look at the systems on our checklist, and consider the underlying messages we would be sending to our teachers if we *did*, in fact, stick to that uninspiring to-do list. We also remembered that we needed to share in the learning *with* our teachers if we were going to cultivate spaces where our teachers felt empowered as learners and agents of change themselves.

Before looking back at our list, we reviewed our goals for the week:

- How did we want our teachers to feel?
- What types of thinking and inspiration did we want to spark?
- How would our time together work toward embodying our campus vision statement?

Then, with our checklist in hand, we considered each item and asked ourselves the following questions:

- What was absolutely necessary to attend to? What were our district expectations that could not be ignored? What were our non-negotiables?
- What could be tabled for discussion until a future date?
- Was everything on this list absolutely necessary? How did our non-negotiables match or align with our goals for the week?

We quickly realized that with a different perspective and slight change in our approach, we could give ourselves more time in the upcoming week to allow for the kind of learning experience we wanted to permeate our school. No longer was the week packed with necessary items to cover. Instead, it shaped up to take a more collaborative, inquiry-based approach—the practice we were trying to provoke and cultivate with our teachers.

Reviewing the year-end reflections from our returning teachers alongside our newly drafted campus vision statement, we brainstormed how we could use those reflections and our vision statement as a springboard for the week. From the teachers' reflections, we discovered a few things:

- Some wanted to know how to use the Ozobots we had purchased last year with the help of a local grant.
- Some were curious about the idea of a makerspace, both how it functioned and what space it actually had in the classroom.
- Others said they didn't feel comfortable with the idea of "free play in the classroom" and wanted help implementing that concept.
- Several said they wanted to infuse more opportunities for their students to be creative in the classroom in connection with the district's curriculum and state standards.
- More than a few still wrestled with how to use questions to guide independent learning.

Knowing that most of our staff enjoyed a bit of friendly competition, we were determined to combine play with a series of activities that would spark the type of thinking we wanted to encourage in our teachers. With that goal in mind, we established the Amazing Maker's Race. The race would include stations located throughout the building that gave our teachers time to explore different materials, provided teachers choice in how they spent their time, and were rooted in the concepts and topics that *they* were interested in.

From technology tools and apps to some basic recycled supplies and even new curriculum resources from the district, we set up stations that were anchored with overarching questions to guide the teachers and support the reflection we wanted them to engage in during their collaborative time together. We also established a hashtag so we could all share our discoveries on Twitter.

On their first day back, our leadership team welcomed our teachers into the library with high energy, excited about where our collaborative inquiry learning would take us. We shared with teachers that they were the inspiration for today's session, that their questions and areas of interest were interwoven throughout all of the week—especially the stations they would be exploring today. We told them that this year would be building off of all of the work we had collaboratively done in the previous school year. Our aim as their leaders, we explained, was to continue to listen and respond to their needs as professionals.

Before sending them off on their challenge, we briefly spent time using a thinking routine to capture initial ideas and questions about the concept of play in their classrooms. We allowed just enough time and discussion to provoke their curiosity and then provided a general timeline for the morning. From there, we sent them off in groups to begin their exploration of the stations we had designed to meet their unique needs, interests, and learning styles.

> Thinking routines are from the work of Ron Ritchhart et al.[2] They help structure conversations to frame thinking in a way that provides equitable space for all learners to explore and express their ideas. To read more about the valuable impact of these routines, check out the Suggested Reading section at the end of this book.

Each station had a set of materials for teachers to explore and a question to prompt their thinking. We encouraged teachers to talk with one another and share ideas for how they could complete the task at that station.

With teachers well on their way, the members of our leadership team dispersed and moved from group to group, listening to the conversations that were happening. We took notes about what we observed and prompted groups with more questions if they got stuck on one particular task or needed a bit of nudging to collaborate with one another. We observed the playful and curious undertone of each of the groups. We heard teachers communicating with one another by asking questions to help make sense of the task at hand at each station, and we watched as teachers tried out resources and tools that they had

Julie Haney, M.Ed.
@JulieHaneyEDU

Maker's Race @SpicewoodPYP #SWESInnovates coding, greenscreen, sketchnoting, makey makey pianos and more! #rrisd1family #itsallaboutMindset

Jessica Vance
@jess_vanceEDU

Amazing Maker Race 2018 has begun. Love getting to see our teachers tinker, play & create. You can't foster an inquiry classroom unless you are an inquirer yourself! #creativity #RRISD1family @SpicewoodPYP @TeyanPageRRISD @tech4fun

shied away from in the past. We celebrated their successes and cheered them on as they completed the different tasks laid out for them.

A few hours later, the groups slowly made their way back to the library for a debriefing session about the morning's experiences. Returning to the thinking routine to anchor our reflection together, we revisited the group's initial ideas about play, highlighting some of their questions and assumptions about this important concept. Teachers shared a variety of experiences from the different stations, naturally making connections between their preliminary thoughts and ideas from the morning to where their learning had taken them by the end of the Amazing Maker's Race. Groups shared about the role collaboration played in their ability to learn different tech tools or make sense of new curriculum resources and textbooks. We asked teachers to share more about this, shedding some light on the specifics of how this actually looked. Teachers recognized that the questions at each station launched them immediately into conversations. They also noted that they had used questions to help make sense of what they were exploring. Making learning a game made them more willing to try new things; they took comfort in knowing that mistakes were part of the learning process.

To conclude our morning's session, we asked each of the teachers to personally reflect on their learning, reminding them that as educators, we would be nudging them to keep an inquiry frame of mind throughout the school year—and that this mindset would continue to structure our approach to learning as professionals. With reflections in hand, we now had feedback for our next steps to support our staff in their learning.

Sharpening the Skill of Reflection

Reflection is a skill, and, just like any other skill, it needs to be sharpened and practiced if it is going to become ingrained in our everyday professional practice. The following six characteristics provide a framework for leaders and educators to reflect on and refine their practice. Used in isolation, none of these translate to a robust reflective practice. When carefully considered and woven together over time, however, these six characteristics help curate a space and culture of reflection.

At the end of each characteristic section, you will encounter *Pause & Reflect* questions for you to consider as a leader. Use these questions to guide your leadership journey. Allow them to provide the space and direction for your personal growth. Additionally, please consider sharing these questions with those you lead alongside. My hope is that these questions spark new thinking, ideas, and perspectives in your collaborative efforts to create a culture of reflective practice.

Relationships

Relationships are important. In both our personal lives and our professional spaces, relationships provide meaning to our lives on a daily basis. Our power, as educators and leaders, comes from the connections we make. Educators at all levels empower others to collaborate by trusting and supporting them and by honoring their desires for deep knowledge and knowing.

The meaningful work and transformation that occurred on our campus didn't happen overnight. It didn't happen as the result of completing the requirements of an inquiry-based approach to teaching and learning. The changes took root because people engaged in meaningful learning together. As we reflected with one another through honest conversations and questions that pushed ideas, we found the courage to try new things *together*. The changes our school experienced would not have had the same level of impact without the foundation of relationship. The work would, in fact, have no meaning if we, as leaders, didn't know our teachers.

Getting to know our teachers as people first allowed us to understand what areas our teachers wanted to explore. Each interaction in the hallway, staff meeting, or team collaborative planning session was an opportunity for us to get to know our teachers and what they were about. We knew that one of our fourth-grade teachers had a passion for gardening and was a master gardener. One of our kindergarten teachers had a love of travel and learning languages. A fifth-grade teacher had a passion for music that filled his days both inside and outside of the classroom. Our art teacher worked tirelessly each year to promote, judge, and organize a statewide youth arts competition in which the students' artwork would be displayed at our state's capital.

We knew these things because **we cared to know more about our teachers**. We were genuinely interested in the things that brought them joy, the things that gave them life outside of their roles as a teacher, and even the challenges and hardships they faced.

Leaders who value their people by listening as they share about what is important to them demonstrate the truth that we are all better together. We, too, learn more about ourselves through relationships that teach us about our role and reveal how we best support teachers and facilitate their needs as lifelong learners.

Designing the Amazing Maker's Race wasn't something we wanted to do for our teachers because it was simply something fun (although creating space for unstructured play for adults is valuable); the idea came from the teachers themselves. Knowing our learners helped us design meaningful experiences for them to explore and investigate tools and concepts. Our teachers felt connected to the learning because we had designed it with them in mind. They felt like part of the learning experience. Through their learning, teachers built relationships with one another, which fostered a sense of community schoolwide. The beauty of inquiry is that it allows a community of learners to collaborate, share ideas, and dig deep into the learning. For this kind of deep learning to occur, however, relationships must be established first. Learners need to know one another first. That knowing leads to the trust necessary to allow learners to be vulnerable enough to share what they might not know,

Inquiry teachers build relationships with their students because they know that, with those connections, they can home in on student interests and passions. They can then encourage learners to tap into those passions to drive the curriculum forward and make meaningful connections to the content. Those who lead with inquiry do the same. We connect all of the parts of best practice with the people we serve and build relationships through the process of honest reflection with one another. Honest reflection requires that teachers feel safe. They need to know they can be vulnerable and make mistakes. We model this value and build their trust in us by being present with our teachers, sitting with them in the learning space, and being vulnerable with them.

* Building relationships takes time. There is no way to rush this process. How do you build and maintain relationships with your teachers and support staff? After you've jotted down your initial thinking here, go ask your staff. What do they say? How does that compare to your thinking?

* Reflect and consider what you know about your staff. What are ways you connect what you learn about them with your campus vision, professional development opportunities, etc.?

* Play allows us all to be a bit more vulnerable and creative. It opens our mindset to explore and try new things. How can you use play to promote bonding amongst your staff?

Curiosity

Thinking is not driven by answers but by questions. Questions, along with reflection, are vital to the process of an inquiry approach to learning. Questions inform the facilitator about what's important to their learner. Questions are a form of assessment that helps us see where our learners are. They can also bring learners together as they engage in the process of sorting through ideas and digging deeper into new questions that emerge when connected thinking takes place.

Leading with a lens of inquiry, we looked at our professional development as an opportunity to cultivate agency in classrooms and across our campus. The goal was to spark innovation within our educational system and to rethink and redefine school norms and approaches to teaching and learning in both our adult and student learners. We wanted our teachers to be curious, to play, to have time to create, explore, let go, and reframe their thinking about their time spent as growing professionals. With that goal in mind, we considered what opportunities we were offering teachers to experience inquiry themselves. We wanted to provoke our teachers to ask more questions, be curious about big ideas, and develop new ways of thinking about their approach to teaching and learning. Collaborating with one another and being willing to stretch themselves in new, exciting ways was essential, which begged the question: How could we spark the type of thinking we wanted our teachers to facilitate with their students that year? How could we get them to explore, play, and tinker?

The makerspace movement in our school had begun to take root the previous year. The foundational values of struggle, problem-solving, communication, creativity, questioning, and research were vital to fostering this movement. Like an inquiry-based approach to teaching and learning, developing these skills within students takes time, intentional planning, and authentic practice as teachers model and reflect on these skills with students.

Simply "telling" our teachers that these skills needed to be included as they developed their lesson plans each week wouldn't change the approach to classroom learning. Teachers needed to experience these for themselves if they were going to be able to pull in a tangible connection to the value of these approaches to learning or the dispositions of a learner. They needed to be able to "feel" themselves as professional learners connecting to their students because they, too, had been given the space to explore things that matter to them. Their voice needed to be honored yet balanced with experiences that challenged them to rethink their approach to their professional practice. We wanted an environment that brought teachers back to the inspired space they felt when they were brand-new to the profession, excited for and open to all of the possibilities of what's to come at the start of their teaching careers.

It is our responsibility as leaders to hold the space of curiosity, inquisitiveness, and uncertainty in these rich spaces of learning. Provocations are an invaluable tool when it comes to inquiry. They encourage new thinking, provoke questions, and frame an overall mindset of curiosity. They are an invitation for exploration and discovery. Provocations can come in the form of an article, video, a headline, or even a question. Provocations are used throughout the cycle of inquiry, nudging inquiry learners to reflect on their thinking, make connections, and dive deeper into the topics and concepts being explored. Those who lead with an inquiry frame of mind propel the learning on campus by inspiring and sparking curiosity and ultimately by being curious themselves.

Pause and Reflect

* Now that you know your learners, how is their curiosity visible in your learning spaces? In what ways do you collect and use their questions to guide your next steps as a learning community?
* Modeling curiosity supports the culture of inquiry we are trying to cultivate. How do you model yourself as a lead learner? How do your learners know what you are curious about?
* How can you tap into learners' prior knowledge and personal interests as a way to nurture curiosity?

Listening

A cornerstone to unpacking inquiry and cultivating a reflective practice is listening. As referenced in the previous chapter, while inquiry is commonly presented as a cycle of learning, an inquiry experience does not need to follow a cyclical process or a sequential series of steps. Through our own experience with personalized learning, we know there is no perfect and clean way it unfolds. Learning is often messy and takes sorting through, both with personal reflection and time spent with others, unpacking ideas, sorting out new thinking, and considering different perspectives. As the cycle of inquiry unfolds, it is the role of the teacher—or, in this case, the leader—to facilitate the learning process through the art of listening. But what does it mean to *really* listen? We all think that we are truly listening, but how do we know if we are really leaning in, soaking up the conversation, and engaging without bias bent toward what we need or want to hear? What are the ways that we, as leaders, can step back and develop the patience to stay, observe, and act with intention, meeting our teachers where they are and not where we think they should be?

In our session with our staff, we used thinking routines to capture the conversations that occurred both before and after the Maker's Race related to the concept of play. These thinking routines played an essential part in the work that took place that morning. Not only did they slow down the thinking and learning process for our teachers but they also provided a framework that allowed us, as leaders, to slow down our listening and really hear the ideas that were being shared and annotate the conversation as it developed.

The role of the listener is not to affirm the learners' thinking or validate initial questions. It is simply to listen. By engaging in the simple act of listening, we modeled the cornerstone of reflective practice. The goal was not to complete a graphic organizer or find places where we could change their thinking. Our job was to be genuinely curious about what they had to share.

We spent the rest of our morning visiting groups, enjoying our time with them, jotting down notes, and vigorously listening to conversations to capture data that could later be used as a tool to unpack thinking or underlying causes—as well as to dig up roots of misconceptions about the concepts we were exploring that day. We honored the spaces of learning, asking open-ended questions and picking up on the questions our teachers were asking, knowing that those mattered most because they were theirs.

And after we had spent time with each of the groups, we gave ourselves some space to share notes, reflecting on the process of learning that had begun to unfold. We made connections to the morning's initial reactions, highlighting questions that came up for groups, noting how they answered many of the questions themselves through their work together. We talked about challenges some of the teachers were still facing and brainstormed some potential next steps or opportunities for which we could allow space in the future to explore some of these ideas. Whether it be at a staff meeting after school or even providing some additional resources and support that teachers could use during their planning time, we were continuing to co-construct our school year together based on the things that mattered to and were much needed by our staff.

With an inquiry approach to teaching and learning, the teacher's role is to facilitate the learning, sitting with their students throughout the process, letting their questions and needs guide the direction and next steps. As leaders, listening provides us the opportunity to collect data to inform our next steps, get feedback as to what our learners may be needing, and mindfully respond in a way that pushes the thinking of all engaged in the learning experience.

As we touched on earlier, listening, similar to reflection, is a skill that must be developed. With that in mind, Chapter 5 continues to explore this foundational aspect of inquiry and the value it holds for leading through this lens.

Pause and Reflect

* What opportunities do you provide your staff to share their thinking with you?
* How do you create a safe environment where teachers feel comfortable sharing their experiences without judgment from the campus leadership? How do you balance this role as their evaluator?
* How can you create a collaborative culture where what you hear can be used to inform your next steps in developing the teaching staff as professionals?

Modeling Thinking and Language

Inquiry teachers intentionally use questions to promote deeper thinking. In doing so, they model the language they want their students to use as they grapple with new ideas.

How do we, as leaders, approach adult learners with a similar mindset? What is our responsibility in modeling the thinking and language we want to see in our teachers and students?

From the tone we set at staff meetings to the way we interact with parents and students within our community, everything we say and do provides cues for those we serve. Leading with an inquiry mindset means that we are intentional with our words and actions. We must model our own curiosities with those we serve and structure our interactions in such a way that we foster a culture of questioning and wonder.

Ask yourself these questions:

- What type of thinking do we want our teachers to engage in with their students?
- If we want our students to inquire about the world around them, explore and dig deeper into ideas, and make connections in their learning, how can we lead with that same lens?
- How can we scaffold our language to support the kind of reflective thinking that is integral at every stage of the inquiry process?

Our August professional development session effectively modeled the type of thinking we wanted our teachers to continue to cultivate as a common practice. We used thinking routines to kick off and end our day, modeling for teachers the value of slowing down the learning process. We also provided a structure to support their inquiry process, a tactic that equips learners to acquire new information and sort through their thinking as they make meaningful connections with the concepts they are exploring.

While teachers were engaged in the different stations, we answered their questions with more questions. This practice laid a foundation for questioning as a means for constructing knowledge and demonstrated how we, as lead learners, settle deeper into the role of facilitators in the learning process. Both the notes we took while connecting with groups of teachers and the graphic organizers we had them use at the beginning of the day were tools that supported us as facilitators of the learning. Pulling back the curtain for our teachers, we explained how we were using their evidence of learning to inform our time together. Although we had a clear objective for the day, their ideas, needs, and questions guided how we responded to them as learners.

Rather than simply telling our teachers that we valued the process of reflection, we intentionally carved out time and space to honor this important part of self-discovery and growth. We showed them how we use questions and language to uncover misconceptions and challenge them to think about their practice in a whole new way.

We continued to model our own reflections and share our thinking as the months progressed, intentionally explaining why we chose certain professional development topics or concepts for future training sessions and continually being transparent about our own reflections as we facilitated the learning process.

- How am I modeling (and making visible) my thinking process?
- What common language do we have as a learning community that supports deeper thinking?
- What systems, experiences, or additional resources do I provide teachers to support the slowing down of the learning process?

Collaboration

As educators, we are a community of learners. Within this community, we can practice the values and skills we wish to instill in the students we serve. We don't have to do the hard stuff alone, nor are we meant to. Collaboration allows professionals to swap ideas, share success stories from the classroom, and explore thinking at a deeper level. As leaders, we can model the value of collaboration by setting up systems and structures for our teachers to be able to come together, share ideas, and build trust with one another through open discussions. Collaboration doesn't mean that we're necessarily tackling a checklist or working on a project together; rather, it can simply be the way we interact with one another to share our perspectives, raise questions, and draw new conclusions based on these conversations. Teachers interact with their colleagues throughout the day. It is our responsibility as leaders to provide a space that values collaboration over cooperation.

What's the difference between collaboration and cooperation? John Spencer does a great job dispelling some misconceptions about these two actions. Scan the QR code to learn more about how we might consider reflecting on these as a learning community.

As we launched into the school year that day, asking our teachers to create and work through something together brought a whole new dimension to the areas they were exploring. What they explored *with* one another led to conversations we could not have predicted or planned. By intentionally structuring the day to include collaboration, we saw meaning making take on a life of its own. Each group constructed their understanding and made their own connections to the content in their grade level, transmitting the learning to something that was more valuable than anything we could tell them was important.

One way we promoted collaboration was through questioning. We were quite intentional with the questions that anchored the challenges at each station, knowing they were a vehicle to promote collaboration amongst the groups. Conceptual in nature, these open-ended questions lent themselves to discussions that allowed teachers to explore and share multiple perspectives. As they practiced collaboration, they experienced community and the power it brings to learning.

Collaboration takes time and space, two things that the traditional daily schedule doesn't allow for in most schools. By creating the conditions for collaboration, we empower our teachers and honor their agency as professionals and as learners. As they engage in conversations and are active in their own learning, they are reminded of the power of collaboration and connection to others. Connection, like collaboration, allows us to seek new opportunities and unpack inequities. Connection builds resilience because help is always nearby, and it emphasizes the power of community. Learning *together* makes us all better.

Central to an inquiry approach is reflection, and while reflection can and should be done independently, reflection with others is also valuable. Collaborative reflection allows us all to reconsider what we already know. In the process, our thinking may shift or transform, or our thoughts may be reinforced. In either case, collaborative reflection reveals a process of learning that is authentic and meaningful to the learner.

To create space for teachers to collaborate regularly, we must be innovative with our days and think outside the box. It will require that we set up or reconsider existing systems in order to make collaborative conversations part of our everyday interactions. We will explore more ways to provide structures that support a collaborative professional practice in Chapter 6, "Making the Learning Visible." For now, though, take some time to pause and reflect on what collaboration could look like in your learning community.

* How would you (or your staff) define collaboration vs. cooperation?
* How do you collaborate? What conditions need to be in place in order for collaboration to flourish?
* How does your leadership style value and support collaboration? What systems (times, schedules, professional development, etc.) are in place that promote collaboration among teachers?

Chapter 3

Dispositions of an Inquiry Leader

Curiosity is one of the first dispositions of an inquiry leader that we'll review together in this chapter. It is also the trait that helped our school's leadership team identify what it is that makes an inquiry leader. We were curious ourselves, and the outcome of our time of exploring and wondering was the discovery of powerful ways to cultivate an inquiry mindset in every learner at our school.

As a leadership team, we were curious about the challenges our teachers faced as they undertook an inquiry-based approach in their classrooms. Listening to them as they spoke about the subjects that gave them time for inquiry—as well as the areas where they feared they couldn't cover all the content—offered valuable insight. Likewise, we paid attention to the questions they had about letting go in their classroom and the concerns they shared about being stretched for time. We listened as they shared their views on using questions as a means of assessment and about how they liked the idea of using questions as a gateway to unlocking rich, valuable, connected learning—even if they weren't exactly sure how to integrate inquiry fully into their classrooms yet.

In a true constructivist mindset, we knew we needed to create the conditions for change. That meant providing opportunities for our learners to play with ideas and construct their own meaning about inquiry as well as space and time to develop these skills. We used the work of Trevor MacKenzie and brought his second publication, the elementary edition of *Inquiry Mindset*, to our staff.[3] We spent an entire academic year digging into the text, testing out new ideas, and making connections to our reading with the work we were doing.

Knowing where our learners' stretches and strengths were, we used "The Inquiry Teacher" sketchnote provided in the book to guide the time we spent with teachers, both in formal planning meetings and informal learning walks. The sketchnote outlines eight dispositions of inquiry practitioners that help create the conditions for meaningful, authentic, and purposeful inquiry to thrive with students. As leaders, we returned to this sketch time and time again, reflecting on the ways

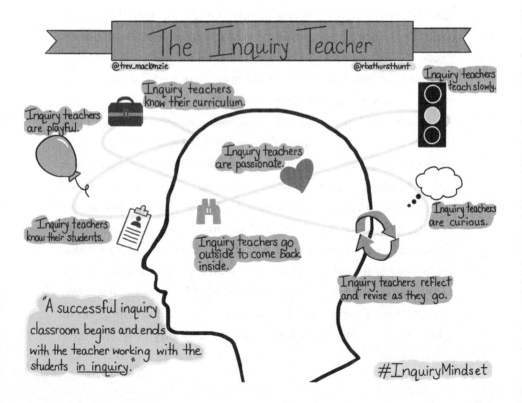

we, too, could embody these dispositions to support our staff, modeling the mindsets we were asking them to take on for their students in their classroom. We found that the more we embodied these mindsets ourselves, the more teachers took risks with their own practice, played with new ways of looking at and planning their curriculum, and honored students as active learners.

We prominently displayed this sketch in our office and referred to it often as we designed and led professional learning on campus. As we added sticky notes to this sketch to document our thinking, we became increasingly aware of the impact that this mindset was having on our campus as a whole. The process of documenting the learning provoked our own thinking as leaders, asking ourselves about the dispositions that are necessary for leading with this lens.

The work of developing teachers as inquiry learners and facilitators begins with an understanding of what it means to embody the dispositions and mindsets of inquiry. So what prevents us from leading with this lens? How do we show up as leaders to fully express an inquiry mindset while not limiting ourselves by the demands and pressures of our roles?

In a contemporary school context, a good leader is one who communicates a clear vision, inspires those they lead to do greater things, assumes an open mindset, is willing to try new things, and carefully balances the managerial aspects of their roles with tenderness and compassion that allows them to relate and connect with their staff. While these assets of a strong leader are all accurate, I ask you to consider a different lens when it comes to leadership.

- What happens to our teachers and students when we assume a mindset that mirrors the practices we are coaching and leading our teachers toward in their practice as educators?
- How can we lead with a lens of inquiry for ourselves and for one another?
- Moreover, what's the significance of leading with this lens?

As we shift our thinking about our roles as leaders and explore more of what it means to lead with a lens of inquiry, our schools will inevitably transform into spaces that exhibit the qualities of inquiry from all sides. Through leading with this lens, you'll experience the following outcomes:

- A trusted community of learners in which we practice a shared leadership approach.
- Engaged learners who find personal meaning and relevant connection to the curriculum.
- Connected and collaborative partners in learning who are inspired and empowered by one another to seek to improve their practice.
- An insatiably curious culture that is committed to exploring more of the *what if*, approaching learning and systems with an innovative and playful mindset.
- The clarity to authentically recognize and harness the power of small steps toward a collective vision, values, and voice in all actions.

Before you continue reading about the dispositions of inquiry leaders, pause for a moment and reflect on the qualities you already embody that reflect a good leader. How do people describe you and your approach to leadership? How do you know this to be true? Consider asking a colleague or other critical friend to describe you as a leader. Use the space below to document your thinking.

Dispositions of an Inquiry Leader

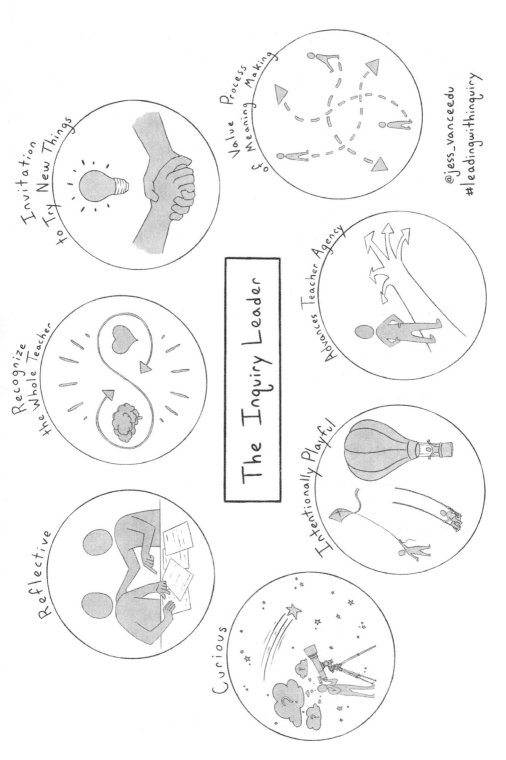

While there are clear parallels between the inquiry teacher and our roles as leaders, our positions require us to explore different expressions of inquiry. In this chapter, we will explore the seven dispositions of an inquiry leader:

1. Inquiry leaders are curious.
2. Inquiry leaders recognize the whole teacher.
3. Inquiry leaders are reflective.
4. Inquiry leaders advance teacher agency.
5. Inquiry leaders value the process of meaning making.
6. Inquiry leaders extend an invitation to try new things.
7. Inquiry leaders are intentionally playful.

The dispositions outlined here are essential for leading with a lens to inquiry. As you delve into each of these characteristics, reflect on how they show up in your role as a leader. Which do you feel are your strengths? Which ones may stretch your practice a bit? And which ones have you never considered before? Pause to reflect and document your thinking.

Inquiry leaders are curious.

Inquiry leaders are compassionately curious about their adult learners' interests, passions, questions, and actions. They remain curious to learn about the ways teachers interact with students. Shifting the focus to questions, inquiry leaders practice asking questions to discover more about themselves and the ways they can support the learning and professional growth of teachers. Additionally, inquiry leaders ask questions to learn more about their colleagues with the hope of building a trusting and safe environment that allows taking risks and trying new things to become a campus culture. Inquiry leaders seek to learn from others—including educators off their campus—and remain curious to develop their own professional practice, stretching themselves to meet their learners' needs. They identify critical friends and others within their professional learning network to challenge their assumptions, shed light on their biases, and push their thinking in new ways.

Inquiry leaders who are curious ask themselves the following kinds of questions:

- How do I use language that shows I am curious about my learners?
- What types of questions do I ask to learn more about them?
- How do I listen to my learners?
- What does listening make me more curious about?
- What interests do I have in my learners?
- How do I include my own wonderings in my professional growth and practice?
- How do I show my staff that I am a curious learner?

Inquiry leaders recognize the whole teacher.

Inquiry leaders give space for their teachers to show up as their best selves. Inquiry leaders create a sense of community and belonging where everyone on campus feels seen, heard, taken care of, and valued. They are mindful of the pressures teachers face and advocate for mindful self-care. Leaders recognize the whole teacher and understand that people have a basic need to feel understood. They invest in their people and find joy in celebrating their passions and interests and in creating a community of belonging. They model the relational approach they want teachers to have with students in their classrooms. Inquiry leaders demonstrate their commitment to the community as a whole by being visible in the spaces of a school. They value getting out from behind their desk to be with their students. Inquiry leaders see *being in the learning* as an opportunity to build meaningful relationships and help create a school culture that is caring and compassionate toward everyone's well-being. Being in the learning means remaining curious with your learners. It means knowing the framework and direction of where you need to go but tuning in and listening to your learners as they guide you there. Inquiry leaders recognize that professional learning does not take a one-size-fits-all approach; instead, like classroom learning, it must be differentiated and value the needs of each learner.

Inquiry leaders who recognize the whole teacher ask themselves questions like these:

- What do I know about my learners' needs, interests, passions, and lives outside of the school building?
- How am I present and visible in our school building?
- How would my learners describe the ways that they feel seen and celebrated?
- In what ways would my learners say that they are taken care of?
- How do I show my staff that I have their needs in mind?

Inquiry leaders are reflective.

Inquiry leaders incorporate continuous reflection into their practice. They reflect on the ways their actions, words, and attitudes impact those they serve. They model their reflective thinking, shedding light on the active process of learning—one that continuously requires the learner to ask questions of themselves and of the learning. While the formal process of reflection may seem like a daunting task, inquiry leaders recognize that their use of language and open-ended reflective questions model informal reflective thinking. Inquiry leaders provide opportunities for learners to provide feedback about their needs. They vigorously listen to the ideas, thinking, and questions being asked. Most importantly, they view this feedback as valuable data that informs their next steps.

Inquiry leaders must practice ongoing reflection to remain adaptable and meet the continually changing needs of their campus and learners.

Inquiry leaders who are reflective ask themselves questions like these:

- How do I use questions and language to model reflective thinking?
- When engaging with my learners, how do I consider multiple perspectives and ideas?
- How do I prioritize space for reflection?
- What structures and strategies make thinking and reflection visible?
- What reflective structures do I model and utilize with staff?
- How do I show my staff that I am a reflective learner?

Inquiry leaders advance teacher agency.

Inquiry leaders trust their learners. They are actively engaged in the learning community, seeking to know more about the needs of their learners by asking questions that empower their voice and direct learning. Inquiry leaders recognize the power of a shared leadership approach, demonstrating the responsibility every educator has to engage and embody the school's vision. They provide multiple opportunities for teachers to demonstrate their roles as leaders, building their capacities as risk-takers and decision-makers who have true ownership of their roles in the learning community. Inquiry leaders encourage and listen to new ideas, challenging their learners to think bigger, and often ask, "What would happen if . . .?" They leverage the power of a shared leadership approach, trusting their learners and actively asking for feedback. Inquiry leaders understand the valuable role that agency plays amongst all learners in the buildings. They know the interests and needs of their adult learners and provide meaningful and relevant learning opportunities to refine and grow their practice. Inquiry leaders provide opportunities and structures for voice and choice that, over time, help cultivate teacher agency in a scaffolded and intentional manner.

Inquiry leaders who advance teacher agency ask themselves questions like these:

- What do I know about my learners?
- How do I provide opportunities for teachers to contribute their voice to their professional goals, growth, and learning?
- What structures are in place that honor the agency of teachers?
- How do my learners know that their voice, choice, and ownership in our learning community are valued?
- Am I doing something for my staff that they could be doing for themselves?
- How do I show my staff that I empower them and value their agency?

Inquiry leaders value the process of meaning making.

Inquiry leaders are patient and understand that rich learning occurs when learners are able to construct meaning on their own. They leverage collaboration and cooperative learning as a means to create space for learners to own their roles in the process of learning. Inquiry leaders infuse opportunities for reflection, understanding the practice's role in the process of learning. They carefully nudge their learners along the way while cultivating a culture that allows for and even encourages mistakes. Those who lead with a lens of inquiry resist the urge to *tell*, recognizing the value of engaging learners in active decision-making and ownership of learning.

Inquiry leaders who value the process of meaning making ask themselves these kinds of questions:

- What are the ways I guide conversations that provide time and space for my learners to make personal meaning?

- How do I demonstrate that I value their thinking, questions, and ideas?
- How do I curate opportunities for a collaborative culture?
- How do I model my own thinking aloud for others to observe and take note of?
- What can I mindfully do to facilitate the learning experience of others?
- How can I model making connections across conversations and the learning I am observing?
- How do I show my staff I value them making meaning on their own?

Inquiry leaders extend an invitation to try new things.

Inquiry leaders remain open-minded to the possibilities that unfold within the natural course of learning. They build a foundation that allows adult learners to feel safe to take risks and fail without fear of judgment. Those who lead with this lens inspire the thinking of their learners through the use of provocations. They invite opportunities for learning through play and understand how to skillfully connect learners' questions to the exploratory interactions they cultivate. They encourage their learners to try new things by asking, "I wonder what would happen if . . . ," while creating space to explore ideas and step outside the traditional role of a teacher. Inquiry leaders model this disposition by sharing what they are exploring and by actively asking for feedback to inform their next steps.

Inquiry leaders who extend an invitation to try new things ask themselves these kinds of questions:

- How do I cultivate the conditions for my learners to feel safe to try new things?
- How can I model my own lifelong learning?

- How do I show my learners that I am open-minded, vulnerable, and excited for the unexpected?
- What happens when my learners lean in and embrace a new undertaking?
- How do I nudge my learners along when they are resistant to trying something new?
- How do I show my staff that I am on my own learning journey with them?

Inquiry leaders are intentionally playful.

Inquiry leaders take a playful approach to learning. Rethinking professional learning, inquiry leaders find immense joy in cultivating spaces that allow their adult learners to take risks, explore, collaborate, and have fun doing it. Engaging in this approach, they see their learners' attitudes toward trying new things soften as they tinker with ideas and explore different ways of doing things. Inquiry leaders approach listening with a mindset that asks, "What can we discover together by trying something new?" They understand that play invites connection and deeper relationship building while leveraging connected learning spaces and a playful attitude. Inquiry leaders harness this disposition to support their outlook and thinking, creating a presence that allows us to change our outlook on things, approaching what's right in front of us with a bit more perspective and open-mindedness.

Inquiry leaders who are intentionally playful ask themselves questions like these:

- What structures do I utilize to engage in play for learning?
- How do I infuse a sense of play into my own professional practice?
- What are the ways I experiment with new ideas?
- How do I learn something in a playful way?
- How do I show my staff that I am a playful learner?

Impact of Dispositions

As you lean into leading with a lens of inquiry, you will foster the mindsets and approaches to learning with a clearer intention to seek to understand. You'll grow your knowledge about how your team functions and how your campus works as a whole. You'll also discover how this approach impacts and changes you and your mindset about leadership.

As you lead with a lens of inquiry, you will observe changes in your teachers, who, over time, will feel empowered to share their voices as active participants in learning. And I'm certain that you will be delighted, as we were in our school, to see their thinking stretched as they approach their professional practice full of curiosity.

The changes we saw in our teachers are worth noting. Conversations that once began with "Yeah, but . . ." shifted to "Yes, and . . . ." Teachers who used to start their planning time with "There's no time to . . ." began saying things like, "You'll never believe what questions my students were asking today!" We used to hear, "I have standards to teach, so I cannot . . . ." As teachers developed their inquiry mindsets, we heard questions like this that led to solutions: "I wonder how we can explore and connect this to the things that are important to our students."

These new conversations reflected a transformation in the culture on our campus—a change that came as a direct result of the dispositions we, as inquiry leaders, actively and mindfully modeled. We saw new evidence each week that affirmed we were changing as a community of learners. Teachers became more willing to talk about *how* they taught and not merely what they taught. They slowly became more reflective, open, vulnerable, and collaborative. The more we became curious about our learners, the more they became curious about their learning. Instead of questions that reflected a culture of compliance, their open-minded, open-ended questions invited curiosity, wonder, and the exploration of "what if?"

During this time, I realized that leaders too often spend time managing—covering the nuts and bolts and tasking teachers to complete assignments and meet district deadlines. I wondered: Were these pressures we felt about meeting expectations creating the trusting and empathetic learning environment we expected each of our teachers to cultivate in their classrooms? How were we balancing our roles as leaders, working within our given systems, yet maintaining a mindset and approach that valued the characteristics of inquiry?

In reflecting on these questions, I realized that, just as our teachers carefully balance their roles in their inquiry classrooms, there's a balancing act that leaders take on as well. We mindfully move throughout our roles to meet the needs of our learners and provide equitable experiences for those in our learning communities. Inquiry teachers understand the depth and complexity of their facilitative role, always putting the agency of their learners first. At the same time, they scaffold the learning to support and stretch their learners where needed and provide additional support to their students for more independence. Inquiry teachers playfully co-construct the learning with their students while being mindful of their curriculum as a structure in the background.

Inquiry leaders play a similar facilitative role. As school leaders, we balance our portfolios by resisting the urge to task and tell; instead, we approach our curriculum and action items with an approachability that invites our learners to be part of the process. Inquiry leaders are visionary and have a growth mindset. They understand the value of structures and systems and create space for all voices to be heard by gathering questions and ideas from their staff. Inquiry leaders are intentional with their words—using open-ended questions, verbiage from the inquiry cycle, and other inviting language that underpins a culture of inquiry. They resist the need to go first, instead pausing for others to contribute to the group while mindfully listening to the ideas that are shared. Inquiry leaders do not feel bound by or limited by time and instead are intentional with *how* they use time to honor the agency of their adult learners.

We witnessed transformational change on our campus with our students and staff because the conditions for inquiry were connected and present in our everyday interactions as a school. While we wore the lens of inquiry in so many ways, we also recognized the tensions and pressures of managing our learning communities. With that reality facing us, the question we had to answer was how we could allow ourselves to unfold and expand to that of an inquiry leader. The Inquiry Leader Continuum provided the answer.

The Inquiry Leader Continuum is a scaffolded approach to the change that leaders experience as they lead with a lens of inquiry. It is a tool that helps leaders reflect on their roles and provides a structure that allows them to be more playful and intentional within those roles.

On one side of the continuum, the managerial leader takes a traditional approach to leadership. These leaders are goal oriented. They create processes and systems to achieve their goals. Managerial leaders do the right things to ensure that they meet expectations and deadlines. At first glance, it may appear that all systems are running smoothly and that any challenges that arise are promptly handled, but something is missing from this leadership approach. You won't find that missing piece in the checklist or as duties assigned, but you will feel its energy as you walk through the halls and peer into classrooms. Managerial leaders produce managerial teachers who focus on covering curriculum and tasking assignments. Getting what they model, they lead a staff that measures the value of their work as a single data point determined by the results of a standardized assessment. In these schools, a culture of compliance reigns. People dutifully show up, but their thinking and results are stagnant.

Leading with a Lens of Inquiry

Managerial Leader

Inquiry Leader

⟵--------------------------------⟶

- Task oriented
- Directs
- Checklist approach
- Controls
- Gives answers rather than asks questions
- Seen as the "expert" or sole provider of information

- Visionary
- Asks more questions than tells
- Value driven
- Risk taker
- Big ideas
- Facilitative
- Less control
- Strong vision
- Listener
- Playful

@jess_vanceedu
#leadingwithinquiry

On the other end of the continuum is the inquiry leader. These leaders are not stuck in the managerial spaces and experiences. They model and balance the complexities of their roles through the art and action of the practice that is at the center of an inquiry framework: reflection. Inquiry leaders move across this continuum, mindfully shifting and fostering the thinking that underpins a culture of inquiry. Their continuous reflective practice allows them to be more aware and present. They make time to think about their thoughts in the quiet space at the end of the day. When they are with other leaders or their teachers, they create space to sit in the learning with their learners. Reflection is the tool that nudges inquiry leaders to ask, "What would happen if...?" They maintain an open mind to the unfolding potential of what they can co-create *with* their learners.

Using questions, the inquiry leader nudges their own thinking in order to approach the managerial tasks all leaders must deal with. Through intentional reflection, they consider how to address the needs of managerial leadership by embodying the dispositions of an inquiry leader. See the table that follows for examples of what that could look like.

If tasked with...	Then consider...
Staff meeting agendas	• How can you playfully gather questions from your staff to frame your time with one another? • How can you start off your meeting with time for your staff to play, connect, and greet one another? • How can you celebrate your staff?
Teacher evaluations	• How can you use language that evokes a softness? • What do you know about your learners and what's important to them? • What are your learners curious about that can more deeply connect their learning and growth?

If tasked with...	Then consider...
Analyzing data	• What tone do you want to set? How can you provoke that thinking from the start? • What thinking routines can you use to structure conversations? • What questions can you ask that provoke thinking and discussion? • What are the areas in which you can celebrate and highlight the work? • How can you embody a growth mindset?
Mandated professional development	• What's imperative? What message are you sending? • In what ways do you connect professional learning to your campus vision? • How can you take a more playful approach? • How can you provoke thinking around a common concept?

As you continue to build trusting and empathetic learning environments that allow inquiry to thrive, I am confident you'll add to the suggestions on the list. I encourage you to share your thinking with other leaders, continue to reflect on your actions as a leader, and lean in further to develop the dispositions and mindsets of an inquiry leader.

Keep the dispositions of an inquiry leader and your personal reflections from this chapter in mind as you continue to read more about the ways we lean in and lead with inquiry. The dispositions are not goals; rather, they are skills to be mindful of and refine over time through a collection of small moves and intentional actions. Take some time to reflect on identifying your areas of strength. Consider, too, which dispositions are a stretch for you. What support do you need in order to grow this disposition?

Dispositions of an Inquiry Leader

> Need some additional nudges as you take stock of your role as a leader? Kimberly Mitchell's Self Reflection Tool may be just the structure you need!

As with all inquiry learning experiences, there may be points of confusion along the way. View these moments of uncertainty as opportunities to grow in your role as an inquiry leader. Use your existing strengths to ground you. Consider which of the seven dispositions of an inquiry leader, with a slight tweak or some intentional focus, could amplify your practice, impacting both your teachers and students.

In the coming chapters, you will find icons depicting the dispositions of an inquiry leader. Take note, as each icon highlights actionable ways you can add these to your practice. Please consider returning to this chapter as you read, revisiting your initial reflections and making connections to how your learning and practice toward leading with a lens of inquiry shifts over time.

> Leading with a lens of inquiry happens most effectively when we employ all seven of these dispositions. Each time we lean into one of these traits, we enhance our inquiry approach, both as leaders and learners ourselves. By making our practices of these traits visible to our teams and teachers, we lead by example.
>
> Use these resources to push your practice and share what you've tried with our community adding your voice to #leadingwithinquiry.

Some of the dispositions may feel more natural to you than others. Revisit the intention you set for yourself at the start of this book and consider how you can stretch yourself as a leader.

* How do your personal inquiry into these dispositions and your role as a leader transform your lens as a leader?
* What would happen if you tried something new or fine-tuned your approach in order to embody an inquiry mindset more fully?

Chapter 4
The Ripple Effect

I've observed countless leaders who excitedly step into their new roles with a vision, an intent to make a positive impact, and a sincere passion for making a lasting impact on a school community. Yet far too often, their portfolio dictates their decisions, and their mindset limits their possibilities. They let their tasks shape their time, and their eagerness leads to quick decisions and a tendency to make changes too soon.

I can think of one leader who exemplifies the opposite. Her values are reflected in her decisions. The way she walks into the building and shows up for the students and staff is grounded in a clear vision. Her actions are well considered, mindful, and intentional. She doesn't go for the quick win; rather, she knows that sustained change occurs when you are patient, committed, and curious. I've been fortunate to work closely and learn from this approach to leadership. Over the course of my years working with her, I've seen what changes are possible when this stance on leadership is embraced.

As campus leaders, we set the tone for the spaces we lead. Our actions, our words, and what we choose to put our efforts toward on a daily basis are a collection of choices. These choices, both big and small, cause a ripple effect. Inquiry-minded choices can foster excitement and empower innovative thinking within a learning community. Conversely, the wrong series of choices can promote an environment in which people act out of scarcity, fear failure, and are unclear about their purpose and goals. As we continue to lead with a lens of inquiry, we home in on the impact of our actions, and we dig deeper to know more about ourselves, what we value, and the things that brought us to our roles as leaders.

Big change-makers and big thinkers do not work alone. They intentionally use their voices, actions, and influence to inspire others to come alongside them and cultivate a culture where the systems clearly reflect the organization's values. These agents of change recognize the need for a unified voice and commitment to making a difference, even as they use their individual voices to spur movement toward positive change.

In the introduction of this book, I shared with you two questions that became the cornerstone of our roles as leaders:

What do you value?

and

Who is a leader?

I want to bring these questions to mind again here as I outline the ways they showed up in our team's approach to inquiry leading and learning. I encourage you to reflect on these questions again as you consider the ripple effect of your leadership.

The start of the new school year always brings excitement. As a leadership team, we begin talking and planning early, anticipating the progress we hope to attain each year.

Whenever new teachers join our schools, we want to be sure they know about the systems that are in place to support them. To that end, we schedule special meetings throughout the year and curate a small cohort for them to be able to connect with one another. We let them know that we will be meeting together throughout the year to support them, listen to their needs as continuously growing professionals, and, most importantly, give them space. We make it clear that we want to celebrate their work with their students and hear about challenges that arise throughout the year. As a leadership team, our intention is to focus on creating the conditions that will let these educators learn and grow. Removing barriers, sharing our knowledge, and asking questions are all tactics we have established to achieve this goal.

We schedule the first meeting in late September or early October to give new teachers time to settle into their routines, meet their students, and begin to feel part of the school community. While it would have been easy to structure this meeting around campus norms or systems, we have chosen to take a different approach. Aware of the culture we want to cultivate with our staff, we start this session by giving the teachers Margaret Wheatley's article, "Willing to be Disturbed."

> I encourage you to take a look at Wheatley's article. Give it a read often, highlight, and take notes. How does what Wheatley proposes impact your thinking?

Because it's still early in the year, and we don't know our new teachers well yet, we don't want to make any assumptions about their philosophies on teaching and learning or teaching styles. We do, however, want to engage them with thought-provoking content that challenges them to think about their thinking.

In the article, Wheatley outlines some key questions that encourage reflection on one's beliefs and values. She calls us all to consider our willingness to have our ideas challenged. Wheatley describes the importance of curiosity and notes that, as educators, we should continue to be curious about others and ourselves. She asks us to reflect on our beliefs and consider how we arrived at these perspectives. She encourages us to step outside of ourselves and unleash the learning that could unfold if given the opportunity to do so.

We provide a thinking routine to frame their reading and ask them to take notes and highlight the ideas that stand out to them. Using these small moves, we slow down the learning again, modeling the way we want to learn together—valuing time but not rushing through the process.

After teachers complete the reading, we open the floor for everyone to share reflections or questions. Teachers usually share stories about students they have worked with in previous years. Inevitably, the ones who challenged them the most also taught them the most about themselves as educators. We also hear celebratory stories about light bulb moments for past students—those special times when things just seemed to come together. Additionally, teachers ask questions and often make comments. Common themes include the realization that they rarely give themselves the space to be curious and that the systems and pressures of administration or parents often take away the fun from learning. These sessions always end up with more questions than answers, which is exactly the point.

> Questions have a way of sparking conversation and reflection that take your learners to new spaces in their thinking. Being mindful of the questions you ask is a critical way to stretch your learners and help them build their reflective capacities as inquiry educators.
>
> Here are a few questions I've found to launch powerful discussions with teachers. Give a few (or all) of them a try and add some of your own. See what comes up in the conversation when you ask thought-provoking questions and then give your learners the time to reflect and the space to ask their own questions.
>
> - What successes are you seeing in your classroom with your students? What do you think has been helpful in getting you to that place?
> - What are you proud of in your practice?
> - What's a challenge you have encountered?
> - What's something you have tried to tackle that challenge?
> - What are your next steps?
> - How can I be helpful and brainstorm some ideas with you?
> - What might you do differently next time?

We wanted our teachers to get comfortable with the ambiguity of learning.

Yes, systems, structures of standards, and district expectations are unavoidable, but when did they become the only things we talked about? What happened to the teacher as a learner? Where was the space that allowed teachers to reflect on their practice as it was happening, not just on the weekends during education conferences or during breaks when teachers had time off? Where was the space that cultivated the curiosity and inquiring minds of teachers?

We wanted to create a nurturing environment, filled with positive experiences—one that motivated and inspired teachers and let them know their work and their time was of the utmost value. Curiosity is the energy of learning, isn't it?

During the session, we ask teachers to think about Wheatley's message and remind them that we will use questions to drive them to think deeply about bigger ideas and concepts not only in this session but all year long. We ask questions not to find specific answers but to show our curiosity about them as educators, as people. We also explain that questions will guide our professional learning sessions throughout the year. No preplanned agenda is set for professional development; our goal is to co-design and co-create the learning we will explore together.

With their feedback, reflections, and time spent with one another, we are then able to curate a space that supports them as learners throughout the year.

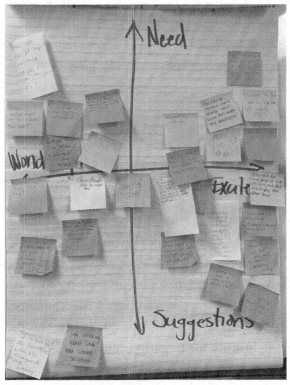

Compass Points Reflection

At the end of our first session together, after we have engaged in conversations, asked questions about systems, and shared resources, we share our genuine excitement about being on the journey *with* them. Before the meeting comes to a close, we ask teachers to use the last ten or so minutes to complete a reflection on our time together. One of our favorite thinking routines to use to get feedback from teachers is called Compass Points. This reflection honors the individual learners by gathering feedback and ideas about how they experienced the learning and asks the learner to consider where we need to go next together. We start with the Compass Points thinking routine because we know it is one teachers can easily replicate in their classrooms to ask their students for feedback. It provides a structure that feels safe for the teacher and models how they could allow *their* students to be co-constructors of learning.

Before we close the meeting, the leadership team spends a few moments showing our gratitude and thanking every teacher for their time, commitment, and honest reflection. We recognize the trust and vulnerability we are asking the group to show us right away, and we want teachers to walk away from this first meeting knowing that we are genuinely curious about them as learners and will support them along the way, always meeting them where they are.

After the meeting, I post the Compass Point thinking routine chart on the wall back in the office. The chart is a visual reminder that every learner on the staff is in a different place. In addition to guiding upcoming sessions, it reveals opportunities for the leadership team members to follow up with our teachers.

The interconnectivity of the actions used to engage our new teacher cohort is not something to be ignored. Creating the conditions for change requires that we, as leaders, reflect on our professional practice and consider the kind of momentum we want to build. We start by considering our roles in provoking this movement and then ask what changes we need to make in ourselves *for the learners'* benefit. Each act in isolation seems small, but they are intimately connected—rooted in our values and the process of inquiry. More to the point, each action creates a ripple effect.

Imagine throwing a stone into a pond. When the stone hits the still surface, you are immediately aware of its impact, fully conscious of the change caused by a single, simple act. Now, let's consider this image as we contemplate the changes we wish to make as we learn and lead with a lens of inquiry.

The sketch on the opposite page illustrates the ripple effect of the simple actions or stones you can use to create change mindfully. Observe the sudden pressure of the initial area where the stones landed. Notice how it reverberates across the surface and causes change across the expansive space. Now notice the collective impact of these actions, the lasting transformation of this space. The undercurrent of these initial actions is compassion and curiosity.

What initially stands out to you about the concept illustrated in the sketch? What connections can you make to your learning and reflections so far in this book?

Values, trust, and professional learning are three "stones" leaders use to create change. And each causes waves that ripple to the far reaches of our learning communities. It is the leaders' responsibility to be intentional with all of their words and actions, especially in these crucial areas. Give yourself time to pause and reflect at the end of each of the following three sections to consider the ripple effect of your actions in these areas as a leader.

The Ripple Effect of Leading with Your Values

Far too often, antiquated educational systems dictate values of performance, conformity, perfection, and end results. Inquiry leaders know, however, that these are not the things that matter most. They are not the reasons that drew you to your role in education. You are in this work for the students. You have big dreams to make a difference in

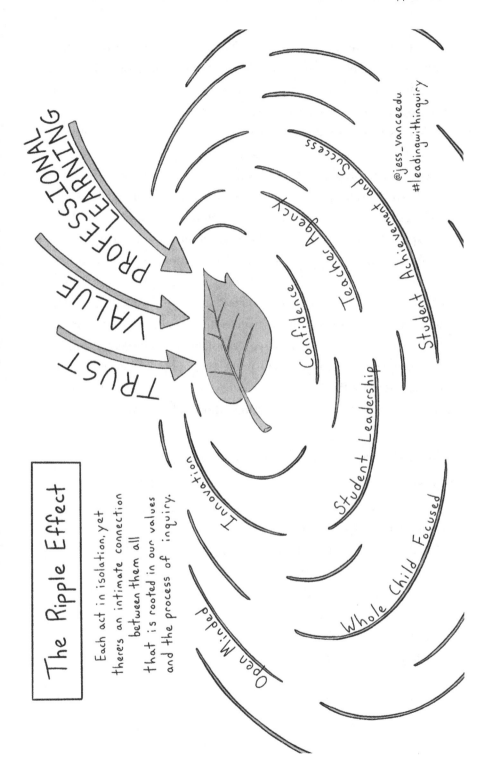

Your core values are not static. Neither will they always be the same as those your colleagues hold. By being clear about what you value most now, you can establish your purpose as well as the way you want to express those values in your actions.

Values are the foundation of your success as an educational leader, but they are not separate from the way you live outside your role at school. The ripple effect of your values impacts all aspects of your life—from the roles you take on personally as a mother, father, sister, brother, or friend to the ones you play professionally. Your core values underpin who you are, what you believe, and how you behave.

You formed your core values over time through a collection of experiences. It's critical to reflect on and understand your core values and how they drive your actions. Below/on the following page, you'll find a few values (some of my own and some from leaders with whom I have worked). Beside each value, you will see possible ways it might show up in your actions and, in turn, the kind of ripple effect it is likely to create. Review the list and consider what values you hold at your core. What possible ripple effects might those values have?

Value: Relationships and Connection	
Manifested Actions	Ripple Effects
• Greets teachers, students, and community at the front door • Schedules time in calendar to meet with teachers without an agenda • Gives teachers open-ended time/space to work on things that they need • Asks for (and uses) feedback about professional development, campus initiatives, etc. • Writes handwritten notes or cards sharing gratitude	• Builds trust • A sense of belonging • Collaboration • Confidence • Shared leadership

Value: Communication	
Manifested Actions	Ripple Effects
• Is mindful of tone, body language, and words when communicating • Provides clear feedback and communication that doesn't leave teachers wondering what's not being said • Invites feedback and reflection and utilizes it intentionally to guide next steps • Celebrates community of learners frequently • Uses questions to invite deeper thinking, provoke alternative perspectives, and learn more	• Trust • Psychological safety • Partnerships • Reflective practice • Gratitude

Value: Joy	
Manifested Actions	Ripple Effects
• Creates moments and opportunities for personal connection with staff • Celebrates learning community • Is present in classrooms, celebrating learning with all students and teachers • Greeting teachers, students, and community at the front door • Learning students' names	• Passion • Fun • Growth • Focused on what's in front of them • Appreciation • Teacher agency

Value: Learning as a Process	
Manifested Actions • Prioritizes time for creative and reflective professional learning • Creates spaces that support a growth mindset • Actively supports teachers in their own professional growth goals • Seeks opportunities for mentorship • Designs professional learning with an inquiry mindset	Ripple Effects • Independent thinker • Knowledge constructor • Build communication skills • Honoring the learner where they're at • Whole child • Creativity thrives
Value: Creativity	
• Actively seeks multiple perspectives • Looks for outside opportunities for collaboration and learning • Playful and energetic approach with teachers as learners • "Yes and . . ." mindset to new ideas • Encourages the transformation of learning experiences in innovative ways	Ripple Effects • Open-mindedness • Risk-taking • Fun • Innovation

Explore the different ways you see these actions impacting the community you serve. Your way of being has a profound impact on others. By showing up grounded in your values, you can be intentional in your actions, including allowing yourself space to make decisions and take action.

As you think about your actions and the values they reflect, I strongly urge you to take a closer look by using this reflection tool from Kimberly Mitchell's book, *Experience Inquiry*. I'm curious what patterns you see after using this resource.

Take a deeper look at what you value. If you have not reflected on your values recently, we encourage you to take the time to do so; we'll be referring to this reflection in Chapter 7.

* How have your experiences influenced what you value now in your career?
* Now consider a meeting, a professional development session you lead, or even the first day back with teachers after a long break. What does that session show others you value? Does it align with your values? If not, what changes can you make to align with what you deeply believe in?
* How can you recenter yourself and allow others to see your compassion through what you value?

The Ripple Effect of Creating a Culture of Trust

It takes time and intention to build trust within a school community. You can cultivate a culture of trust by balancing your vulnerability with authentic leadership. Being open with those you serve while showing your curiosity about and compassion for them as people first are all traits that contribute to a culture of trust.

New teachers want to make a good impression on their leaders. Knowing that about our incoming staff, we realized they would be putting forth their best selves and might be guarded at times. As we launch into our first year together, we want to create an environment that encourages each of our new teachers to feel welcomed and safe. With that in mind, we intentionally set the tone that our school would be a safe space for them to not only teach but also learn.

Our focus on curiosity and reflection establishes the expectations we have for a learning environment built on continuous feedback. We ask for their ideas and dig deeper into their thinking and questions. We use structured thinking routines as well as simple questions, such as "How did it go?" or "What did you think about what we worked on today?" to show that we deeply value their roles in the learning.

Establishing expectations is a foundational aspect of building trust. By being explicit with our intentions (clearly outlining our goals at the beginning of each session), we repeatedly identify and then model our core values as we refer to their questions to drive conversations and put them—the learners—at the center of the learning. We then build on that foundation using the framework of curiosity, the disposition that drives the inquiry-based approach.

Curiosity is essential, both for the students and for educators' professional practice. We use the Wheatley article for the first session with our new teachers because it highlights the role curiosity plays in learning. It also allows us to compare the inquiry approach to the outdated educational systems we work within. Those systems, in which questions have been traditionally used as a tool to elicit a single right answer, demand teachers quickly check for understanding and then move on in order to stay on schedule with the allotted scope and sequence of the curriculum. In contrast, an inquiry approach to learning honors the natural way each person learns.

Leading with this lens of inquiry—setting the expectations and modeling the dispositions of curiosity and reflection—shifts your role as the leader from the "sage on the stage" to the "guide on the side." As the guide, you lead by modeling thinking and asking questions. Rather than seeking the *one* right answer, leaders ask and value all types of questions because questions take *all* learners down a rich and meaningful path of authentic discovery.

Reflection is at the center of the inquiry cycle. It is central to the process of learning as learners construct understanding while building on the foundation of their knowledge. In order for this learning to occur, learners must be honest with themselves, reflecting on what they know and don't know, in turn seeking more understanding through asking questions, conducting research, or connecting with others to help make meaning of what's being explored. The same can be said with the relationship between reflection and trust.

As you reflect on the trust level in your learning community, consider the following questions:

* What opportunities do you create for yourself and your learners to reflect on how everyone's actions impact learning?
* Are you vulnerable enough to ask for feedback?
* How can you use curiosity to inform your next steps for meeting your learners where they are while stretching yourself as someone who leads with a lens of inquiry?

In addition to curiosity, reflection, and vulnerability, accessibility and feedback are essential to building a culture of trust.

Accessibility

Most leaders understand that accessibility and trust are important. As an inquiry leader, however, you will need to be intentional and innovative in the way you integrate them into your professional practice. The more you lean into gathering feedback from and being accessible to your learners, the more you see your teachers take risks and trust you in your roles.

As an inquiry leader, you take an active role in the learning process. Instead of simply managing people and systems, you act as a facilitator and partner in learning. You can do this by identifying experts in your building (both leaders and learners) who drive everyone to improve. Inviting others to contribute to the learning, asking questions, and listening to your learners as you seek feedback will inform your next steps as you lead your campus. The ripple effect of this collaborative approach is that your students will see the way you work with teachers and will begin to view partnerships in learning in different ways than a traditional school system elicits.

During our first meeting with our new-teacher cohort, one of the intentions we share with the group is the way we will be visible in the school. Explaining that role in classrooms goes well beyond formal observation and evaluative purposes; we are there to engage in conversations with students and come alongside teachers. To that end, we will regularly ask students about their learning, curious to hear about their thinking and what connections they are making. We will also pull up a chair next to teachers as they construct weekly lesson plans based on student questions and feedback. We are there to celebrate student learning, co-teach lessons, and provide additional support for teachers who are trying something new. We attend grade-level meetings, are visible in hallways as students are moving throughout the building, greet teachers at the door as they walk into the building for the day, and invite teachers into our offices beyond scheduled meetings.

In short, we set the expectation that the leadership team will be present and visible because we value the collaborative efforts of an inquiry community. Over the past few years, we've seen that the more present we are, the more teachers view us as a valuable asset to their learning. We become true partners in learning and receive invitations to classrooms not only to celebrate students but also because we are seen as a resource to support and enhance their professional growth. Teachers ask for feedback about their practice, and we then engage in a collaborative conversation with one another, driven by their questions and interests. We ask more questions than we provide answers, creating space they need to draw their own conclusions, make personal connections, and honor their agency as learners. We learn more about what our adult learners need and the things that are important to them because we are visible and we are able to best plan our next steps as leaders because we have a pulse on what's really happening in our classrooms. With continuous accessibility, we model the role of a curious inquiry leader.

Feedback

An inquiry leader understands that trust begins and ends with a partnership in the learning in which the leader, teacher, and student are actively engaged. Communication drives the learning for all participants. Through listening, language, and questions, inquiry inherently unites us.

Feedback is the data that informs next steps in facilitating learning and in growing professionally as a leader. As you lead with a lens of inquiry, it is vital to withhold assumptions and judgments and, instead, be curious about what learners are sharing. Listen for what is being said as well as for what's not being said. Consider what is missing in the sharing and where your learners may be holding back.

Listen for questions. They explicitly tell you what your learners need and will help you identify trends among your learners. Repeated questions provide a clear direction for your next steps as a leader. They may help you see where professional learning needs new technology tools or where reflection strategies could be better used in the classroom. Repeated questions also give you insight into ways you might want to approach your role differently so you can better meet your learners' needs.

> Honor the voice of your adult learners. Consider using the Staff Reflection Survey from Kimberly Mitchell's book *Experience Inquiry* as a tool to gather authentic feedback from your staff to help inform your next steps as a leader.

As you solicit feedback, be intentional with your language. Create a comfortable space and develop a shared trust, using statements that begin with "Yes, and..." or "I wonder how we can..." Follow questions with an open ear, honoring your learners' ideas without judgment. Ask open-ended questions to push thinking and then pause longer to give your learners space to develop their own ideas. View feedback as a form of reflection.

Continually model the dispositions of an inquiry leader by noticing and being mindful of any and all feedback. Pause and remain present by asking yourself, *What is actually happening here*? As an instructional leader, you are there to give your teachers feedback, and feedback goes both ways. When you act on the feedback your learners share with you, you communicate to them that you value their voices.

Infusing thinking routines into professional learning sessions by creating surveys and other check-in opportunities allows teachers to express their needs as they share their thinking. Remain open to their feedback and respond creatively. Resist the urge to align your responses with systems and procedures or to rely on logistical thinking and a managerial approach to leadership.

Think back to when you were a teacher in the classroom and students answered questions incorrectly. Rather than shutting them down, you likely thanked them for sharing as a means of encouraging them to keep thinking. Adopt a similar approach with your adult learners by welcoming feedback, which fosters trust in the learning partnership. Use their feedback to co-construct learning. Stay open-minded to possibilities and remain playful in your approach while working within the constraints of the systems you work in.

Ultimately you will sharpen your skills when you view feedback as an opportunity for personal reflection.

Pause and Reflect

* Are you accessible or available? Are there unseen barriers keeping people from letting you into their part of the learning process?
* How do you actively seek feedback from your staff about your role as a leader?
* How are you visible to your learners? Do they seek you out for feedback?

The Ripple Effect of Inquiry in Professional Learning

Sessions like the one described earlier are opportunities to cultivate change and inspire greatness within your systemic limitations. As you lean further into leading with an inquiry-based approach, you will want to plan and approach your time spent with learners.

Leading with a lens of inquiry requires reimagining your role in developing your teachers by rooting yourself in inquiry. Rather than telling teachers what they "should" do, you view them as learners with their own interests and strengths and identify ways to stretch them.

Many inquiry educators have inspired me through the years, but none more so perhaps than Trevor MacKenzie and Rebecca Bathurst-Hunt. Their contributions to the inquiry community have deeply impacted my view on our responsibilities as inquiry educators and leaders. Their work sheds light on the role that teachers play in an inquiry-based approach to teaching and learning and lifts up the ways we honor the agency of our young learners throughout the learning process. If you are familiar with their written work, *The Inquiry Mindset: Elementary Edition*, you'll notice many parallels to the ideas presented here. The dispositions of an inquiry teacher align with those who lead with a lens of inquiry. We embody these characteristics as leaders because we, too, are inquiry teachers, facilitating learning through an approach that puts the learner at the center of our focus.

I mentioned earlier that their sketchnote of the Inquiry Teacher is always visible in our offices. We return to it often as we reflect on our approach to leading the learning with an inquiry lens to our professional practice. The sketch illustrates eight different characteristics, highlighting the pivotal role each plays as educators facilitate learning with their students and further develop themselves as inquiry teachers. Here, I want to focus on two of these traits because of their potential to create a ripple effect with our adult learners and their students: *Inquiry teachers go outside to come back in* and *Inquiry teachers are playful*.

From off-campus field trips to the Apple store to a morning spent at a local museum to learning walks on other school campuses or even within the walls of your building, one way to inspire adult learners is to allow time and space for exploration and discovery. By going outside their classroom walls, they are often inspired to learn something new and to make connections to what they already know and do. Time spent away from students is valuable in that it fosters the teachers' curiosity and wonder.

Likewise, cultivating spaces of play is valuable because it builds community, risk-taking, curiosity, and learning. Whether you provide physical materials or manipulatives for your teacher-learners to explore or use thinking routines as a structure for the tinkering of new ideas, play grows and empowers curiosity. In your role as a facilitator, encourage deep thinking and ask powerful questions that evoke discovery. Allow time and space for richer, reflective thinking—and for play.

Just like teachers are required to address standards in their lessons, you can set standards for your approach to professional learning, ensuring that it connects to their questions and their areas of interest while maintaining your vision and mission. You may be wondering how to take your *must-do* list of requirements and reframe it through your lens of inquiry. Questions always provide the answer. Below is a list of questions our team considers each time we design professional learning experiences with our adult learners:

- What opportunities have we provided for our learners to play?
- In what ways are we sparking curiosity or provoking thinking and questions?
- What questions are essential as we facilitate the learning?
- How and when are we allowing the space for our learners to reflect?
- What feedback are we using to drive our actions?
- What do we already know about the dispositions of our learners? What are their strengths and stretches?

- How do our learning experiences reflect our values?

Planning Professional Learning with the Inquiry Cycle

Just as the inquiry cycle suggests, each learning opportunity begins with a provocation that sets the stage for active and engaged learning. From there, the intent is to design experiences that tap into a creative space for teachers to play and explore. By intentionally building in opportunities to construct personal meaning through reflection at every stage, learners build this essential skill that is far too frequently neglected with more traditional approaches to professional learning.

> As you recall from Chapter 2, provocations invite the learner into the learning. They promote wonder, curiosity, and personal relevance. Provocations can be videos, artifacts, picture books, or even going outside into nature. When designing your provocation, consider the needs of your staff, their interests, and what type of thinking you want to inspire in your learners. Scan the QR Code to access a few ideas to get you started!
>
>

As our leadership team leaned into inquiry in the professional learning that occurred in our school, our view of our roles in the process of inquiry shifted. The inquiry cycle became our structure for everyday guidance as well as for more formal professional learning opportunities. Intent to uphold the curiosity and ambiguity that is essential to learning, we continue to make learning visible for our teachers by relying on the inquiry cycle to sort through difficult ideas with them. We use their questions while we consider ways for them to construct the meaning. And we work through the uncomfortable moments that arise when we don't have an answer for them or we are unclear about our exact next steps.

 I've included here two different agendas or planning templates we used to apply the inquiry cycle to our own professional practice. In each of these samples, we are explicit with the process ourselves and orient our learners to each of the stages in this cycle of learning.

We have seen the ripple effect of applying the inquiry cycle to professional learning move through our school in several ways. In planning meetings, teachers share openly about how the learning unfolds in their classrooms. With practice, they become more confident and adept at allowing student questions and interests to direct the learning while keeping the conceptual focus of the unit in mind.

Teachers also engage in true collaboration with their teammates, asking hard questions of one another. They reflect on their personal practices and are open-minded about taking risks with their student learners, not holding them back because of their own fears of letting go. We hear conversations about all types of data. From formal assessments to student reflections and anecdotal notes about teacher observations and documentation of student conversations, learning becomes more about what they are doing *with* students instead of what they are doing *to* students. Their conversations are focused on the whole child, the process of learning, and their roles in providing an equitable learning experience for every one of the students they serve.

As you practice and embody the mindset of an inquiry leader, you, too, will become aware of the ripple effect of your actions. In some areas, you may see subtle shifts, disruptions that nudge your learners to think differently about their students, their professional practice, and themselves. In other areas, your efforts will create cultural waves that completely flip the thinking and approaches to teaching and learning in the classroom.

You will notice growth, too, in yourself as you empower others. Lean in. Get to know your learners better. Carve out space to slow down and think. Enjoy riding the waves and celebrate the impact they have as you create the conditions for inquiry to thrive *together*.

Pause and Reflect

* Based on the professional learning experience we shared at the beginning of this chapter, what do you think we valued? What makes you say that?
* Think about a leader you look up to. What ripple effect did their leadership have? How do you know what they valued?
* How do you give feedback to your learners? In what ways do you consider what you know about your learners to differentiate your feedback to meet their needs?
* How do you get feedback? What impact does this have on your next steps as a leader?

Chapter 5
Leading Is Listening

To listen is to lean in softly with a willingness to be changed by what we hear.

—Mark Nepo

In the traditional sense, the role of leadership is top-heavy, but it is about more than making a single voice heard. As you lead more with a lens of inquiry, you'll find that a shared leadership approach allows you to continue to be curious and to be deeply connected to yourself and the people you serve. Leadership, then, becomes about bringing out the best in yourself and the best in others in pursuit of a positive purpose.

Let's now return to one of the characteristics of cultivating a reflective practice: curiosity. I've found that by being curious myself, while also understanding the dual roles that listening and questions play in conversations, it is possible to drive learners and myself toward honest reflection and growth.

When you are personally curious about something, you will delve into the topic with intense thinking that often starts with one question and leads to many more as you uncover answers and make connections to your prior experiences. The process transforms your thinking.

The question then becomes: How can you create the conditions for curiosity to thrive in the environments in which you lead?

Planning connected learning experiences that provoke thinking and wonder is the answer. With that goal in mind, inquiry teachers infuse student voice, choice, and ownership by getting to know their students and using their passions, interests, and questions to co-plan and co-construct learning experiences and assessment opportunities.

Teachers need to experience similar learning opportunities. As instructional leaders, we can't expect teachers to infuse inquiry into their practice if we don't give them the space to engage with it themselves. We honor their agency as learners in the way we listen and lead. When you get to know your teachers and discover what they are curious about, you can co-design powerful professional learning opportunities with them. The end result is that, through your engaged and shared leadership, you empower them in their relationships with students.

Listen to the Learner

In addition to curiosity, one of the core characteristics of cultivating a reflective practice is listening. But how do you develop or expand your capacity to listen deeply? With so many things that vie for an educational leader's attention, how do you ensure you are actively listening while remaining open to differing perspectives, seeing the world as others see it, and continuing to be attentive while refraining from judgment?

In this chapter, we'll explore why it is important to rededicate energy toward listening. You'll also discover ways to be more intentional with *how* you listen.

It can be easy to insert your judgment or agenda when listening, wanting to steer a conversation in a certain direction to solve a problem or make a point. While it's important to lead with a bigger vision and perhaps the end in mind, it's also important to allow the space for the questions to come, for others to share, allowing them and *yourself* to go to unimagined places. As you lead by listening to your adult learners and building relationships with them, they will begin to understand that you are there to help them grow in their practice. This trust enhances their capacity for risk-taking and innovating. By rededicating your energy toward listening and being more intentional with HOW you listen, you will be better able to keep reflection and inquiry at the center of your leadership.

Below I'll share several stories that highlight different ways our school leadership listened to our learners. Through the experiences and reflective questions we asked ourselves, you'll better understand how your own inquiry mindset impacts your learners. Consider using these questions as a way to connect my experiences to your learning community. Ask yourself which of these resonate with you as you begin to reflect on the ways you listen.

"You Just Listened to Us . . ."

It was springtime and the end of our school year. I was rounding out my first year as the campus International Baccalaureate (IB) Coordinator. I scheduled time to briefly meet with all grade-level teams and specialists to hear their final reflections and gather feedback about how they experienced the school year with me. During our last meetings, we sat in a circle, and they answered these questions as they shared how they felt about the school year:

- What things could we celebrate about our students?
- What did they find out about themselves as professionals?
- What goals would they like to focus on in the new school year?
- What systems or structures did they find value in and want to see less of or more of?

Using a Plus/Delta table on chart paper so everyone could see, I tracked the conversation, jotting down their exact words, feelings, and takeaways. I would occasionally ask for someone to explain answers more fully, wanting to ensure I wasn't making any inferences about their honest feedback and reflections. My intent was to prevent my personal biases from impacting what I was hearing. As our time wound down, one teacher asked to share a final reflection.

She said, "You know, you just listened to us this year. That's exactly what we needed."

While there's always a part of me that wants to know more, the timing of her comment was perfect. Instead of asking for more, I simply smiled at that teacher, shared my gratitude for her generous words, and responded, "That's what I am here for."

After the team left, I sat with that comment for a while—not because I wanted to relish in the good feeling of positive feedback but because I wondered what was happening *before* I joined this team. What stood out about our time together that made her feel like the previous leadership and administration wasn't listening to her? How did I approach my time with her and the other teachers that showed them I was listening? What messages was I sending through my words, tone of voice, and body language?

Listening Shapes the Learning

District initiatives and campus goals drive the direction of a campus and help unify the focus of a community. After our district purchased new devices for each of the elementary campuses, the instructional leadership team was tasked with the goal of increasing technology integration into the curriculum. With that goal in mind, we spent time early in the year mapping out formal professional development opportunities and potential curriculum connections, as well as ways we could introduce new tools to our teachers. Each time we sat with teams for extended unit planning, we'd return to this list, offering suggestions for how these technology resources could be integrated into their units. We had built a community in which risk-taking was valued and innovation was celebrated, so our teachers were used to our questions and gentle nudges.

During one curriculum planning session, a colleague asked a team of teachers how they thought they could offer their students some opportunities to explore technology within the unit. A simple question, asked many times before, was not received so well this time. What we expected to be a brainstorming session that included the exchange of ideas about some of the apps we had already tried or even new tools that the teachers had previously expressed interest in exploring erupted into a cacophony of frustration and overwhelmed chatter by the group. Aware of the pressure from our leaders to ensure the teachers were integrating technology into multiple learning experiences, our initial feelings of surprise and desire to fix the situation washed over us.

Instead, we sat back and listened.

We listened to the teachers tell us that their classes were already struggling with simple tasks like logging in to their computers. We listened to the ways they felt pressed for time to prepare for the upcoming standardized tests and how juggling all of the different technology tools at once was just too much. We listened to even more sharing about the additional pressures they were feeling from administration and how these changes overwhelmed their already full plates. We listened with genuine curiosity to understand their perspective and learn more about what they were experiencing. We allowed the space for all of the fears, frustrations, and anxieties to emerge from the group. Listening to what was being said made it quite clear that our agenda wasn't what was needed at that moment.

Without dismissing the challenges they were facing, we brought the conversation back to them, meeting them where they were yet not allowing those fears to hold them back as learners themselves. Valuing the risk-taking it took to share these frustrations, we acknowledged their feelings before adding one more question to the conversation: "So—what *can* you do?"

We saw this moment as one in which our stepping back would allow them to step forward, informing us where they needed to go and honoring their agency, voice, and role in the ways we supported them.

Needing to wrap up the meeting, we made a list of things the teachers needed to feel successful. We documented their ideas, including us going into classrooms to teach alongside them, having additional time to explore the tools on their own, and scaffolding lesson ideas to meet the needs of their students. We closed the meeting with new, co-constructed plans that were so much more powerful than if we had not involved our teachers in the process.

As I walked back to my office, I reflected on the experience with these questions:

- What was present that opened up the conversation and moved it in the direction that it went?
- How did listening shift the way we were leading the learning?
- How did we know what was needed at that moment?

Share Their Enthusiasm—and Frustration

The busyness of the morning can be quite consuming. From students, parents, teachers, and substitute teachers arriving in the building to the preparation for community speakers, assemblies, or other scheduled events, the arrival of the day is full of distractions and requires a constant refocusing of attention.

As leaders, we start our mornings at the front doors of our school building, greeting students, directing visitors, and, quite often, fielding questions and needs from teachers who are settling into their day. We value being present, being visible, and being available to whatever needs or opportunities bubble up.

One Monday morning, several teachers stopped to check in. One shared about a conference she had attended the previous week and her excitement to integrate the resources she learned about into one of her upcoming units. Another teacher walked up with a grin on her face. She was excited about her upcoming summer trip to Bali, as well as the training she would be completing that would certify her to teach yoga. Just before the morning bell rang, a first-grade teacher stopped to share about the success she had the week before using a new technology tool that would earn her a tech badge. She and her teaching partner would be trying it that day with her class.

As my colleague and I listened to these teachers share their enthusiasm, we noticed the curiosity they expressed. Whether it was a story about learning to use iPad apps to allow students to produce their own green screen videos, a passion for yoga, or exploring new tools with students, the pride in their accomplishments was obvious in their eagerness to share their joy with us in the most modest yet inspiring ways.

The excitement for the things our teachers were exploring and learning about, both inside and outside of the building, excited us! We relished the time each of them took to stop and share their aha moments, accomplishments, and wonderings about next steps as learners. We asked questions to learn more about their new adventures, expressing our curiosity about their passions and lives outside our building. My colleague and I both made mental notes to follow up with these teachers and check in on how they and their students were doing. We wanted to be intentional about encouraging them to try new things as they proceeded in their journey as learners alongside their students.

Inspiring moments like these filled our mornings, but plenty of moments were not as celebratory. There were moments of stress when the district's internet wasn't working right before a big presentation in the library or moments of frustration when a teacher called in sick at the last minute and we had to scramble to sort out the students and plans for the day. There were moments when we listened to the anxiety a teacher faced regarding the data meeting that was scheduled that afternoon and other moments when the failures from the previous day hung heavy on a teacher's mind.

We knew that each time we paused to listen was significantly important. We could feel it. Even so, I couldn't help wondering the following:

- What compelled teachers to stop on a busy morning just to tell us some good news?
- What interactions had we previously had with each of these teachers that allowed them to be vulnerable and share so much with us?

Unpacking the experiences above brought several reflective questions to mind and sparked countless conversations about the importance of listening. Both the listening and the reflection revealed that we, as the leadership team, valued the relationships and dialogue we had with the teachers. Over time, our actions built trust with our learners and informed our next steps as leaders.

In the examples I share, it's the collection of the ways we show up for our teachers that was important. From informal connections in the hallways to being actively present in our classrooms, all of the ways that our teachers and students see us do matter.

Our teachers trusted us enough to tell us the things that were troubling them because they knew we were listening. They felt the psychological safety to ask questions and share their feedback about the systems that were in place and trusted themselves enough to try new things because they knew we were listening without judgment. It's the collection of all these moments and actions that demonstrated how we value them.

Listening is a skill that takes time, effort, and intention to improve. Your daily interactions with others allow you to practice this skill, observing how it impacts your relationships as well as the way you see others and yourself. You can show up for others by listening, valuing, and being curious about the things others share.

In the more formal interactions, like planning or faculty meetings, it's important to participate in the conversations actively as a listener.

Tune into ways you can support your staff. What you hear from them can and should determine what levels of support they need. If you listen, they will tell you whether it would be ideal to collaborate with other leaders or participate in coaching opportunities. Take cues from what they say to design future professional development sessions.

Attentive listeners are . . .

- Inquisitive
- Empathetic
- Patient
- Open
- Resistant to the urge to interrupt
- Asking questions at the right time to gain understanding

Although listening is an internal action, your body language, responses, and even your questions let people know you're paying attention. Below I'll share how our leadership team made questions an intentional component of attentive and effective listening. I'll also explore what to do with the information and knowledge you gain from listening in order to better support your learners.

Just as teachers use their classroom spaces to anchor the learning with student-created products, chart paper can be used to document the big concepts being explored. Using sticky notes to capture questions and thinking, you can create a space for ongoing reflection and growth. My colleague and I made these tools visible in our office, as it was the space our learners came to often for help, and we wanted them to see themselves within that space.

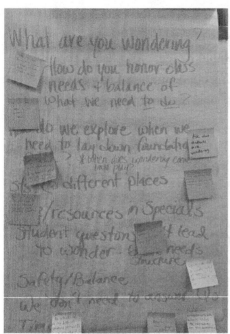 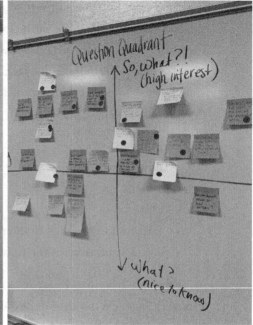

Curious about possible connections to what was being shared in our collaboration and interactions with teachers, we created an office workspace for ourselves that would support our own reflection as educational leaders and enable a type of productivity that was energized and forward-thinking. In our offices, we would debrief our conversations with teachers and ask each other reflective questions to consider intentions, reservations, and connections more deeply. We would share notes about the questions that came up for teachers, attach sticky notes to anchor charts from professional development sessions we'd previously led, and post a colorful graphic onto a space we fondly called our Idea Wall. In doing so, we were engaging in meaningful reflection as leaders, which guided our decisions moving forward.

These visuals provided gentle nudges for us to maintain focus, identifying connections throughout the school year. But what we also realized was that this collection of work showed the teachers that we were listening. Maintaining a visual workspace that displayed their words and ideas conveyed a clear message to our teachers that their voices mattered and that they were the ones who continued to remain the focus of our time and our work. While not always neat or Pinterest-worthy, the learning process unfolded as we used *their questions* and *their ideas* as a guide for the ways we collaborated throughout the year.

After our own self-reflection as leaders, I realized one important commonality with how we approached team meetings, individual time with teachers, or other professional learning sessions. We came with the intention of curiosity—a desire to understand our learners, meet them where they were, connect to where they needed us the most, and honor their individuality and agency as learners. This created a collective strength as we partnered with our teachers, working together as a whole for the success of our students.

Building the Capacity for Questions

Inquiry teachers facilitate conversations through mindful listening. They stretch thoughts by introducing new perspectives on concepts being explored through provocations. They group and regroup students, asking questions to guide the learners' thinking toward discovery and meaningful connections.

The ultimate goal for educators is to nurture the whole child and to give them the best opportunities to prepare for their futures. Grades, assessments, reading levels, and standardized test scores garner lots of attention from stakeholders but are only one measure of education. Inquiry leaders strive for more.

As we lead and model with an inquiry approach, we are mindful of our tone and genuinely interested in what teachers are sharing. We noticed our language made a difference in the way we guided conversations and allowed others we engaged with to feel psychologically safe, take risks to try something new we had suggested, or be open-minded and vulnerable enough to vocalize the change in their thinking. One way to model this disposition is through the use of questions. We let go of the idea that asking a question is a means to an end of a thought or assessment of what's been understood. Instead, these questions bring us together as a learning community.

As leaders with an inquiry mindset, we also let go of the fact that we always need to know the answer or what's next and be open to the feeling of not knowing what step to take next. In doing so, we show our teachers that we, too, are participants in the learning, curious about what we're exploring together, yet confident that together we can create engaging learning experiences for students and develop a solid foundation for professional growth and development. We build the capacity for questioning in our schools through our own practice and our own reflection, continually moving toward spaces that honor the learner, their voice, their needs, and their passions.

Here are a few ways I have used questions to empower our teachers and flex our own skills as we lead with a lens of inquiry.

What Makes You Say That?

A resource I quite often recommend—and even provide for teachers to help them begin to shift their roles from "sage on the stage" to a facilitator of inquiry learning in the classroom—is the work of Harvard Project Zero and Ron Ritchhart.[4] Time and time again, I've seen the impact that thinking routines have on students in the classroom, empowering them as learners while providing the scaffolded structures and frameworks they need to slow down the learning and make their thinking visible. (We'll dig deeper into these routines in Chapter 6, "Making the Learning Visible." For now, here is one routine to help highlight how intentional questioning can impact our roles as leaders.)

What Makes You Say That? is a thinking routine and question that prompts an intentional pause in the learning and has an impact on both the student and teacher. This question challenges the learner to think more deeply about their thoughts. It prompts them to make connections or question their own thinking. This thinking routine also provides the teacher the opportunity to listen actively. We find that this question models the type of thinking we value while we are building our own capacities as listeners. It provides us the same pause we need to be better reflective listeners. By asking this question, you can begin to lead with an inquiry mindset.

Give it a try and see how it shapes the conversation and the way it impacts how you listen.

> While *What Makes You Say That?* is a useful question to ask, some educators share that this statement may reinforce stereotypes around sensitive themes when our knowledge about that topic is still developing. As with all questions, our tone and body language impact the way others perceive our inquiries. Some alternatives to try include the following:
>
> - Can you share what evidence you have to support your conclusions?
> - How do you know this?
> - How can you be sure of what you are saying?
> - Can you explain how you worked that out or came to that conclusion?

The Question Formulation Technique

The Question Formulation Technique (QFT) is a questioning framework that supports the building of questioning competency. Dan Rothstein and Luz Santana's powerful publication titled *Make Just One Change*[5] outlines the process in a step-by-step structure that is easily implemented in a variety of learning contexts. If you haven't experienced the QFT, I highly recommend you try it.

I use the QFT to help teachers develop their questioning competency so they can, in turn, support students in the same manner. Creating the conditions to generate questions that will shape next steps *together* has powerful ties to co-designing and co-constructing learning.

The QFT is widely supported by a community of educators who share resources, strategies, and guiding practices at the website rightquestion.org. Templates, lesson planners, and step-by-step guides are a few examples of the rich takeaways I have accessed in this space. I have used this technique in a variety of ways with the adult learners I support because it creates the conditions to more fruitfully collaborate and connect.

Question Another Question

Curiosity begins when a question is followed by a pause that makes the learner want to know more, dig deeper. A leader's natural inclination may be to respond to the questions with a correct answer or opinion; what's more meaningful to the learner, what supports their construction of knowledge and understanding, is to scaffold their thinking along the way.

Not everyone is comfortable with the idea of questions. In the traditional model of school, questions are viewed as a form of assessment for understanding what's being covered. As such, many learners are conditioned to fear asking and answering questions. Consider how often have you heard the phrase, "I know this is a stupid question, but . . ." Even though *everyone* has questions, most people are fearful of asking for clarity, and no one has all the answers.

If you haven't routinely included questioning in your practice, one place to begin is to follow a question with another question. Following up an inquiry with another question allows you to pause and go deeper, exploring and tuning in to what's behind the questions being asked. The same can be said for the learner.

Make your follow-up questions specific to what's being asked. Asking questions of the learner helps guide them through the possibilities versus telling them the options. It is okay to suggest possible options to the learner gently; however, a question in return supports ownership of what's being explored by the learner. Likewise, their response provides you, as the leader, with a strategy to co-construct the direction you are headed together.

When teachers ask me about what possible picture books might best launch a unit of inquiry or inquire about the best types of artifacts to collect for students' digital portfolios, I quite often follow up with another question. I ask them questions that encourage them to think more clearly about their purpose, intention, and goals. Sometimes the questions offer some potential options, and sometimes the questions require teachers to rethink what they've already done or have already tried.

Of course, the types of questions you ask will change depending on where the conversation is headed or what's needed at that moment. What's important is to remain curious. While brief, here are a few question stems and sentence starters I heavily rely on and share with teachers as I coach and support them to explore their facilitator roles in an inquiry classroom.

- What makes you say that?
- How do you know?
- Can you tell me more?
- I'm wondering . . . ?
- Have you thought about . . . ?

Here is a resource for you to help bring these questions to life in your practice. This PDF is a simple reminder of these question stems that you can print off and attach to the backside of your staff ID badge. Now you can have these clear stems at the ready anytime and will be able to put questions to use in shaping the learning in your interactions with others.

Using questions like these offers a unique way to approach reflection. Slight shifts in our approach to inquiry impact the entire learning community.

Promoting Discovery and Insight

Teachers ask countless questions in their classrooms each day: questions about the characters students are analyzing in their most recent book they are reading aloud together, questions to check for understanding of the math strategy they are exploring, or questions that launch big conceptual classroom discussions.

Just like an artist mixing different colors to find their perfect shade of green to illustrate the rolling hills in their landscape, there is an art to asking questions. Effective questioning requires balance for both open and closed questions. Too many closed questions can shut down a learner's thinking. A powerful essential question can lead the learner down a path of research that illuminates new ideas and ignites new passions, and even more questions.

To explore this idea with those who are new to teaching with an inquiry approach, I often start with a short video that models how questions are used in our classrooms. James Nottingham's "Learning Pit" video clearly illustrates how the intentional use of questions impacts learning in the classroom.[6] Before and after this video, the teachers and I engage in an open dialogue using thinking routines and documenting the conversation as it progresses. I ask them to make connections to the ways their thinking has shifted after viewing the clip and give them space for reflection on their personal teaching practice. This brief yet provocative video opens the door to a reflective conversation about our roles in the classroom and the ways our intentional use of language—in this case, questions—promotes the type of thinking we want to see in our students.

> Have a watch now! This eleven-minute video is full of questions that spark your thinking and ignite your curiosity!

In the previous chapter, we shared that one of the necessary elements needed to cultivate this reflection is intentional use of language. I am a big fan of Bright Morning and the work of Elena Aguilar. Her approach to transformational coaching parallels that of inquiry—putting the learner at the center of the work, focused on meeting them where they are while keeping the bigger picture in mind, knowing when to push forward or even when to pull back, providing additional support and structures as needed.[7]

If you are familiar with Aguilar's work, you're already aware of the extensive focus she puts on the types of questions leaders use as we coach our teachers to reflect on their educational practice. Questions have the power to transform the way they view themselves as teachers.

The purpose of cooperative conversations is to skillfully make suggestions that move the learner in ways that are necessary, yet never forced, for their growth. Through reflective listening, you can facilitate conversations that allow learners to discover and construct personal meaning to their work instead of telling them what they *should* do.

By empowering your teachers to own their learning, you help create a culture that values the agency of all learners.

While there are endless ways you can use reflective questions to move the learner forward, here I've included some guiding question prompts that may help you explore the way you utilize questions as a way to encourage and prompt reflection.

Instead of this...	Try this...
How did you decide to group your students into their leveled reading groups?	What thoughts did you have that prompted you to make those changes in your leveled reading groups?
Is there something that is helpful?	I'm curious to know if there is something that's helpful for you to...? What do you think?
Why did you choose...?	I'd love to know your thoughts about...

Feeling challenged and "stuck" with something that did not sit well with you	I was reflecting about . . . and wanted to revisit . . .
Saying no to something you disagree with	I would love to challenge your thinking . . .
Teacher fixed mindset	I wonder what would happen if . . .
Telling	I would like to be playful in the way we . . .
Don't do it that way. You need to . . .	I would like to nudge you to consider . . .
Why don't you . . . instead?	I'd love to challenge your thinking in a new way.

Try flipping language in your questions. What do you notice happens to the way your questions are received? How does this promote more reflection and growth on their end? How do these types of questions change you as the listener?

Coaching through Questions

When you want students to build their comprehension skills as readers, you model your thinking as a proficient reader or use rich literature to illustrate the way language comes together. These intentional teaching moves shape students and develop the skills they need to be fluent readers. To continue to build the comfort and culture of questions among our staff, you'll want to follow the same method.

As teams of teachers are meeting during their planning time or are engaged in professional development sessions with one another, we listen to them as they share. We spend time pulling in the words and asking ourselves, *What am I hearing? What am I feeling as a result of these words?* Then, we sit with it and process.

We give ourselves the small space to practice reflection and decide what's needed.

- Is an open-ended, reflective question necessary to guide the conversation in a new direction? Or, perhaps, a more explicit question is needed to give me a bit more understanding of what's being shared.
- "I'd love to challenge your thinking here . . ." is a stem I often use to nudge a learner's thinking a bit further. When I'm stuck, or perhaps even unclear about my learner's thinking, I return to the question, "What makes you say that?"
- Sometimes I don't say anything at all. Much can emerge in the silence when you give learners time to think. Notice what arises in the stillness of those moments and take note of what's not being said.

You will read more about the role of questions and how to specifically use them as a means of leading, facilitating, and coaching throughout the inquiry process in the next chapter.

Pause and Reflect

* What are your personal experiences with questions and the role they play in learning, coaching, and supporting teachers?
* How do you listen? Are you a good listener? What makes you say that?
* Now, bring to mind someone who is a really good listener. Are there any? Perhaps only a few? In your notebook or journal, jot down the qualities that first come to mind about this person. What words or actions surface for you?

Chapter 6
Making the Learning Visible

Inquiry educators document thinking by capturing the learning as it unfolds and highlighting learners' voices in the classroom. Sharing student portfolios and other authentic work displays with a variety of audiences creates a sense of community. The more we connect and make clear that we value their voices, the more we build trust. Students see themselves as part of the process of learning, owning their roles in this process, seeking to understand themselves more authentically. Through all of these efforts, teachers celebrate their students' learning.

One of the many benefits of inquiry—both for adult and student learners—is the celebration of the process of learning. Slowing down learning and listening to your learners' questions honor the unique direction they drive you. Unpacking big concepts together, facilitating reflection, and supporting learners as they identify personal goals and growth celebrates their dreams and progress.

Leading with a Lens of Inquiry

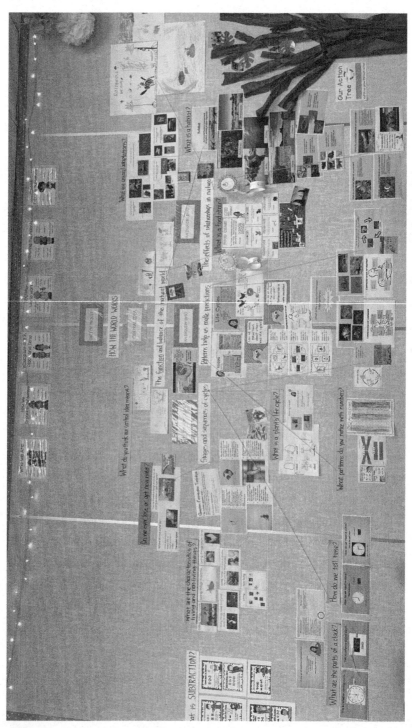

Source: Ana Hoang Spicewood Elementary, Austin, Texas

More Than Just Four Walls

As a former inquiry teacher in the classroom, I looked at Julie's and my office as a space to celebrate the process of learning. We wanted to cultivate thinking, conversations, ideas, and reflection among our learners as well as model the ways physical spaces can be part of the reflection process of learning. We also wanted to show our student community that their teachers are learners, too, affirming that learning happens with each and every one of us in our community of learners.

Using part of the large open wall in my office, I tacked up sticky notes from exit ticket reflections, ideas we were exploring together during a professional development session, a picture of the book we were using during our campus-wide book study, and our campus vision statement. As the guide for our work together, the vision statement took the most prominent place on a bulletin board.

We wanted to anchor the unfolding of the learning journey that was taking place, consistently making reference to this space, calling out particular artifacts, and inviting the teachers to engage in conversations to make connections to what they saw posted on our walls. During sessions with our new staff, we modeled the ways we physically took their questions down from our learning wall to guide our time with them. While they were constructing their personal meaning between the different artifacts, we would listen to them share and then add their reflections to the anchor charts. They were using this space as learners themselves, finding the value in making the learning visibly unfold right before their eyes.

We, too, returned to these artifacts of learning as we prepared for individual coaching sessions or brainstormed action plans to support district initiatives. Along with our anecdotal notes, we viewed this documentation as valuable data that informed our next steps with our learners. We would analyze these displays as we continually reflected on what was needed to meet the teachers where they were at, differentiating the ways we approached our roles, leveraging our time in the way that best served the growth of all learners.

Having this space also lent itself to collaboration across the campus. When teachers would drop by the office, something on the bulletin board invariably drew their interest. Prompted by their curiosity about what they saw, they would ask questions based on another artifact of learning that we had intentionally placed from another grade level. On a typical school campus, there is little time for interaction, let alone collaboration, beyond a grade-level or department meeting. School days are planned to the instructional minute to ensure that mandated instructional times are met and adhered to.

But with this documentation of the authentic inquiries generated by the teachers themselves, we began to see collaboration and conversation happening across grade levels. Primary teachers shared with us that they may have never thought to reach out to a fifth-grade teacher, never once considering that these different age levels of teaching and learning could impact one another in this professional way. Other teachers felt inspired by some of the resources and ideas explored by another and scheduled some time to visit that classroom to learn more about it firsthand during one of their planning periods. This wall not only documented the learning taking place by our faculty but also provoked other educators, nudging them more toward collaboration, an underpinning of an inquiry practice.

Looking outside of ourselves promotes perspective-taking and encourages innovation, both qualities we hope that our teachers infuse into their daily classroom routines and learning experiences with students. Another way we work to make the learning visible is by leveraging the power of tech tools that bring our educational communities together and, in turn, grow our professional learning networks. These networks, however, are not limited to the four walls of our classroom. We find them at the different conferences we attend, within our own school districts, and on social media platforms such as Twitter or Instagram. The collaboration and connection with one another allow us to play with new ideas and provoke new thinking within ourselves. It's what helps us grow ourselves in our practice as educators.

As we visit classrooms and walk down the hallways, we take

Julie Evans
@msevanspyp2nd

Oil spill clean up happening in fm 101! Second grade scientist working together to clean up the mess. We are learning how our actions are impacting our environment.
@SpicewoodPYP #Sharingtheplanet

photos to document learning and celebrate the amazing work being done by the teachers and students. We snap pictures of teachers working with students, capture images of hallway or bulletin board displays, and tweet quotes from what we hear during our visits as we ask students about their learning experiences. We add hashtags on our posts to connect with one another as a school community (as seen during our back-to-school session described in Chapter 2), making the inquiry visible beyond our office space.

Hashtags are a great way to connect learning communities around a certain topic. We create unique hashtags that support campus-wide goals or use hashtags to help us connect with other inquiry educators and leaders. We celebrate learning in a way that honors the voice of our teachers, empowering them to share their thinking and their questions with a greater audience. Through this sharing, our teachers experience what it's like to document their learning, practicing reflective thinking as they determine what artifacts they'd like to capture along the way.

Making the Learning Visible

We use social media platforms to celebrate our school communities and to grow ourselves. We make our learning visible to learners, modeling the types of language, thinking, and questions we want our teachers to begin to consider. Staying curious, we collect ideas and resources from other inquiry educators and leaders. We reflect on the ways these connect to our own practice, bring them to the table when meeting with other leaders, and share them with our teachers during planning meetings, informal classroom visits, or coaching sessions. We gain perspective by stepping outside of ourselves.

Kellie Keating
@keatingkellie1

Ready to share w/ parents at our Learning Celebration! Did a great job sharing our Free Inquiry projects w/ friends. Really great presenting & listening by all. Wonderful way to practice communication! We felt a bit like our 5th grade buddies at exhibition #SWESinnovates

Leading the Learning

EdCamp

Another way we celebrate our learners and make the learning visible is by letting them actually plan and lead the learning. We create and maintain spaces of agency that lift up teachers' voices to share success stories from the classroom. We invite educators to teach their colleagues about the ways they integrate outdoor learning experiences into their lessons, structure their lessons as they expose students to a new technology presentation tool, or facilitate independent inquiry projects. As leaders, we let go of the need to brainstorm, plan, and facilitate

Advances Teacher Agency

all professional development, instead highlighting and celebrating the amazing things we get to experience as we walk into classrooms or conversations we encounter as we are walking the halls and attending planning meetings.

By adopting an EdCamp philosophy to professional learning, we shift the power of leadership toward a more collaborative, shared approach. In Chapter 4, we looked at ways professional development can model the inquiry approach to teaching and learning. The EdCamp model takes this approach to another level.

There are multiple ways to facilitate EdCamp; however, the basic principles are the same: Teachers teach one another, and participants choose the sessions they'd like to attend. At the start of each school year, we ask for feedback to learn more about the ways teachers want to grow professionally. We keep a running list of different things we see in classrooms that might be helpful to the group and simply ask teachers if they have something that they'd like to share with their colleagues. We keep these lists displayed in our office, reminding us of the "experts" in the building.

When it comes time to plan professional development or schedule learning walks for new teachers or other visitors to campus, we can easily return to these lists. By creating systems like these, we show our teachers we value their role in the co-construction of learning for our campus as well as the part they play in the process. Sharing their knowledge and expertise allows the community to see the strengths of their colleagues. It also allows us to reflect on the learning and action our teachers have taken based on their growth.

Inquiry Cycle as a Frame for All Learning

We want our learners to be inspired to do something with their knowledge, change the way they approach their learning, or think in new ways. Ultimately, we want our learners to take action based on their learning. So it's not a surprise, then, that "action" is one of the final stages of the inquiry cycle.

We introduced the inquiry cycle early on with new staff members and referenced it heavily during our planning sessions with all teachers. Even so, we noticed that our teachers were struggling to apply this framework to their planning time outside of our sessions with them. They could talk about the learning experiences as they related to each of the stages, but the depth and complexity of its application in the classroom were lacking. Student questions were being collected but not integrated into the active learning in the classroom. Learning experiences felt disconnected, more like a checklist of activities to be done *to* students. They spent time "covering topics," even though it was quite clear that a majority of the students had mastered the work the year before. This misalignment caused us to inquire more into the disconnectedness of this framework and its application in the classroom.

While the framework illustrates our natural approach to learning, its ambiguous nature means that there is no one way to put it into practice. We knew that our teachers could better integrate this approach into their daily practice if they were the ones experiencing it themselves.

Any time we introduce a new thinking routine or technology resource, we put it into the hands of our teachers, providing them the supported space to construct their own confidence and knowledge surrounding it. With that in mind, we knew that we needed to be more explicit with how we were using the inquiry cycle with them as our learners. We needed to model the flexibility of this structure, adjusting and modifying where needed while facilitating a larger vision.

We took action with small steps at first and gained momentum the more we prepared agendas or planned learning experiences for professional development sessions. We were intentional with how our language, both written and verbal, and digital and physical spaces supported this model. Our slide decks called out each stage as we were engaged in them. Whether we were tuning in to initial thinking with a provocative video clip or magazine headline or making connections to some of our research about different ways we could integrate SEL (social-emotional learning) experiences into our district curriculum requirements, we leaned into the discomfort with each of these stages. We shared our thinking with our learners, letting them know when the learning "didn't go" where we expected but how we were still able to integrate their needs into our larger vision as facilitators of learning.

What better way to sit in the learning and get a true understanding of an inquiry framework than structured time spent with teachers using the inquiry cycle. I shared two sample agendas with you on page 78. Consider revisiting these resources with a fresh perspective on how you spend time with your learners.

By printing a large poster of the inquiry cycle and adding it to our learning wall, we reinforced the value of making learning visible while practicing an approach to learning that puts the learner at the center. As we had been with other artifacts in this space, we were intentional with the different references we made to it during curriculum planning or coaching sessions. We attached sticky notes to show our learners where we were in the learning, connected the questions they asked to the different stages in our learning, and explicitly revealed the ways we connected their interests and passions to the different stages of learning.

Source: Callie Janosky Bluebonnet Trail Elementary, Austin, Texas

The more small moves we made with our learners, the more impact we saw affecting the classroom; for example, we witnessed students using language from the inquiry cycle. During my daily classroom visits, I talked to fourth-grade students who shared that they were sorting out their research with a partner, working collaboratively to determine what next steps to take. I sat with groups of first graders who were digging into a new unit, generating questions as they tuned into the concept of resources. I saw the teacher guide the students through a question sorting activity, beginning the co-construction process of their unit. Across a grade level, the classroom displays differed depending on where the inquiry took them as a group. No longer were the hallways lined with perfect, "Pinterest-worthy" bulletin boards or photocopies of the same worksheets. The learning was unique, a fact that became clear to the students themselves!

As we continue to lead with a lens of inquiry, we model how we use the framework to approach our work with their learning. We intentionally use the language of inquiry by highlighting the different stages with our learners, helping them see the *why* behind our actions and approach to leading the learning. We pull back the curtain, showing them that we are in this together.

Leading with this lens means that we always come back together to reflect and process the learning. This action is just as valuable as all of the time spent in classrooms or time preparing for professional development. We unpack the learning, asking one another questions about the things we noticed, sharing our notes, and determining possible next steps. We connect with our admin team, making suggestions for continued support or connections between our observations and campus or individual teacher goals. We view this time as one that provides the documentation of what we are learning about our learners.

Documenting Your Learning

Leading with a lens of inquiry means that you, too, are engaging in your own inquiry journey. It means you are practicing the characteristics of an inquiry teacher, so your learners see what is possible with this mindset. How do you document *your learning* during this process? What are the ways you record what you are learning about your learners? How do you use this to inform your next steps or connect to your campus goals or your district's vision and mission?

I've outlined several ways you can support the learning by making the journey visible through learning wall displays or social media sharing. In this section, I want to highlight how we collect data and document observations with our learners. The data you will collect—in the form of notes, classroom visits, and multiple opportunities for feedback surveys—will inform your next steps.

Learning Walks

Informal visits or *learning walks* provide an opportunity to be curious, connecting with your learners in a way that shows you value spending time with them. Whether I am visiting on my own or leading a group on a learning walk, I make sure to let the teacher know that we are not looking for anything in particular.

When you visit a classroom, walk in with a smile. Say hello to the students. Sit on the carpet during small group instruction or pull up a chair beside students who are working together on a project. You can take a pen and paper to document your thinking or snap a few pictures to capture and celebrate learning with your community.

Visits, done repeatedly, build trust. They provide an authentic peek into classroom learning and help you get to know your learners so you can identify the best ways to support them.

Inquiry Journals

One of the tools we use in our school to guide professional learning is an inquiry journal that documents our thinking and our questions. This space reframes our thinking as leaders and tracks the journey we are on with our learners. An inquiry journal symbolizes for us the pause we need in order to slow down the learning and engage in an authentic process that balances the needs of the learner and the bigger picture. Just like we do when we lay the groundwork of curiosity, we model using inquiry journals by utilizing this practice ourselves. Eventually, modeling leads to a practice that becomes our default response no matter the scenario.

Source: Marwa Nsouli, International School of London, Qatar

One of the ways we've seen our own reflection transform is how we document our thinking in our inquiry journals. We make notes about what we are observing in our learners, mapping the ways the conversation is unfolding and, perhaps most significantly, the questions that arise within us during this time. Leading with a lens of inquiry means we continue to be curious about our learners and what they are interested in. By documenting our notes as questions, we reinforce this quality. We pause, lean into silence and uncertainty with a bit more ease, and shift our thinking about the way that questions always need an immediate answer.

As with any inquiry, there are times when we don't know how things will unfold. We trust our learners, carefully observing conversations, assessing needs, and readjusting plans as needed. Documenting our thinking through questions has a way of slowing down time. As teachers contribute to group conversations or we're engaging in an individual coaching or mentoring session, we document the questions that arise for us. Sometimes these are related to systems or daily tasks or action items, and other times they lend themselves to questions about challenges our learners are facing. We return to these questions later on our own. We also bring them to the table when we meet with others in our leadership team.

The questions push us to document our observations in a unique way. We can sort through our questions and find common themes to connect to the overall vision of our campus. Sometimes we remind ourselves that questions don't always need an answer; it is the process of asking them that supports the way we construct knowledge about our learners.

Shared Documents

Collaboration is an underpinning of inquiry. It's what allows us to access different perspectives while we sort through big ideas, connecting with one another and learning at a deeper level. Therefore it's also important that, as leaders, we model this quality and bring forth a common language to our learners. We use shared spreadsheets and docs to help us collaborate while we maintain our individual campus roles. We bring these into weekly leadership team meetings, reconnecting ourselves with our learners while adding individual perspectives and actions taken to support them toward growth. We create spreadsheets to track teacher and team goals and use forms and surveys to collect feedback directly from our learners. Documenting what we are observing and hearing from the learners themselves provides us with the multiple perspectives needed to make decisions as we move forward.

Using shared resources, we become better attuned to one another, noticing the cause and effect of each of our independent moves but observing the bigger impact this has on teachers when we can approach our learning in an aligning way. We use shared documents like these to plan for professional development, brainstorm and prepare individual coaching sessions, and determine plans for budgetary spending needs.

We use our collective voice as leaders to amplify the message that we are all in this together.

The multiple ways we document our learning provides an ongoing conversation that reminds us that the natural process of learning is quite messy and unclear at times. It reminds us to remain curious and observe what's right in front of us. We leverage our roles as leaders by documenting the learning in innovative ways that connect our learners and a professional learning network that gives new perspectives that stretch all of our thinking. We maintain our roles as inquiry leaders, intentionally documenting the learning *for* our learners, scaffolding opportunities for deeper thinking while mindfully facilitating the learning as it unfolds—even when we are unsure of where our learners will take us.

Pause and Reflect

* What are the ways teachers know you honor their voice, choice, and ownership in the learning?
* How can you use the physical spaces in your building to make the learning visible? How do you get everyone involved in making the learning visible?
* How does your campus vision and mission connect to your work? How do you make this visible to all stakeholders?

Chapter 7
Nurturing a Culture of Inquiry

Inquiry is a mindset. It's a stance we take. It's an intention we set for ourselves, our teachers, and our students because it honors the natural unfolding of learning.

Our current educational systems neglect this mindset by focusing on performance and perfection over process. It's an inequitable system that leaves our teachers and students feeling undervalued and uninspired.

Far too often, we fix our mindsets to meet the demands of the system. We feel the weight of its pressure and never-ending expectations, acting out of response and fear of underperforming and continuing to perpetuate the thing that's incongruent to the natural way we all learn.

How do you nurture a culture of inquiry given these pressures? Where are the spaces that allow you to move and impact these systems intentionally? How do you, as a leader, cultivate a culture that works to include and honor the agency of learning?

The collection of ideas, stories, and actions shared within these chapters embody a mindset that recenters *all* learners on the exploratory nature of learning. This approach to professional practice leads to specific constructivist values, allowing them to grow and flourish.

With an inquiry mindset, there is no need to feel defined by the systems you work within. Rather, it is the responsibility of leaders and educators to redefine the pivotal roles we all play in the process of learning and cultivating a culture of inquiry.

Leaders cultivating a culture of inquiry are like gardeners working in a flourishing garden—one that is interconnected, diverse in nature, and teeming with robust life. Gardens are complex environments. As the gardener, you must not only be knowledgeable about the basic structure and function of plant life but also *work with* the native environment in order for the plants to thrive. You may plant seeds that do not sprout and may need to provide additional care and support to a particular harvest. Occasionally, you may experience resistance from external factors beyond your control, like excessive heat or a season with abnormally high rainfall. Nature demands the gardener's attention to the present moment. As you tend to the constant and ever-changing needs of these spaces, you must carefully observe and respond to the needs of what's right in front of you while being steadfast in your vision of what's possible when you work with the natural elements life gives you.

In the same way, all of the elements of inquiry are interconnected. If soil is still a foundational piece in a garden, there must be a balance of nutrients and moisture that provide the initial structure that allows seeds to grow. One must carefully monitor and test the soil for a healthy environment that's capable of nourishing and sprouting life. So if soil is a foundational piece in the garden, what is the foundation in our educational spaces?

The people.

The people and the mindsets of those who teach and lead in our schools are what make it flourish and grow. It is the people who work to develop our schools as environments rich in learning opportunities, cultures that abound, and responsive to the diverse needs of our communities.

Nurturing a Culture of Inquiry

In the previous chapters of this book, we've explored the power of a shared-leadership approach in our schools of inquiry. As leaders, it is our responsibility to create the conditions that allow this type of shared-leadership culture to thrive. We shift away from our roles as managerial leaders solely operating from response mode toward leading with an inquiry lens, understanding the bigger picture, and maintaining the vision for our learners the same way that the master gardener uses their garden design. We build strong foundations that cultivate a culture of inquiry by planning with the end in mind, remaining intentional yet open-minded toward change and being curious about the unexpected possibilities that naturally unfold.

The purpose of a garden is to provide the food we need to nourish our bodies. Through tenderness and mindful attention, the gardener nurtures and cares for their seedlings. The gardener provides what each plant needs to mature and yield a bountiful harvest. We do the same with our students in our schools. Our teachers nourish students' minds by carefully selecting meaningful learning experiences that give them the skills they need to be independent learners beyond the walls of the school building. Structures are provided for students to find a love for reading, seeing literacy as a doorway to their future pathways and careers. They nourish students' hearts by spending time building classroom communities, digging into students' passions, and creating spaces that provide opportunities to practice communication and self-management skills during group projects, time spent outside, and unstructured play. They develop critical thinkers who are not afraid of failure, who see a misstep as an opportunity to try again and learn something new, and who infuse our values of constructivism as a framework for the schools we build. Our traditional school systems are not built on these values, and yet, how do we leverage our roles as leaders and work within the system to nurture these values?

The Values of the Constructivist Educator

As leaders, we must focus our attention and nourish the qualities and characteristics we wish we see within our students by addressing the needs of our adult learners. In Chapter 4, we explored the ripple effect that our values have on our actions in our roles. Knowing our core values as leaders makes a significant impact on how we reflect on our actions, make challenging decisions, and bring clarity and awareness to our roles as leaders. We are clear on our core values and actively practice the values of a constructivist educator to continue to nurture a culture of inquiry in our schools. Through these values, we invest time to model and maintain spaces that honor agency, curiosity, reflection, and collaborative learning. Although these values have been gently explored throughout the book, let's take a closer look now.

Agency

As leaders, we co-construct the learning with our learners by providing structures and space that give them voice, choice, and ownership over the learning. We nurture and care for a culture of inquiry by recognizing the roles each of us plays in the learning community. We value the active participation and contribution of our learners and carefully notice the questions that arise, listen and look for the ways they respond to what's unfolding, and use this feedback to show us the direction that we take together. We lean heavily into our vision statement—creating this with our teaching staff and referring to this statement often—re-grounding ourselves and our learners about the "why" behind each of our actions. This statement doesn't just adorn the hallways or lifelessly live at the top of our weekly agendas but provokes our thinking and drives the decisions we make to support the professional learning for our teachers and the opportunities we provide for our students and learning communities.

Like the essential questions that guide our units of inquiry in the classroom, we return to and reflect with one another on our campus vision statement, noticing the direction the learning has taken us. As leaders, we saw our intentional use of our vision statement show up in our classrooms in many ways. Teachers used the statement as a provocation to launch rich discussions amongst their students to establish classroom-essential agreements at the start of each new school year. They stretched themselves and their capacities as leaders by advocating for new programs and resources for our students and stepped forward on their own to lead on-campus professional learning sessions.

We make plans as leaders and guide our schools forward using this vision. We scaffold and support our teachers and continue to honor their agency in each of the big and small moves we make. And while this practice gives us clear direction and purpose, it also re-grounds us together in the process of learning. There are many ways I have observed and supported schools that honor the agency of their teachers. With reflections and feedback from the teachers themselves, below are a list of ways that our adult learners felt valued. Each of these, of course, needs focused attention, active and ongoing opportunities for reflection, and feedback from and with the learners to authentically meet the needs of the unique community of educators.

Ongoing feedback and weekly check-ins: These can be a series of a few questions that differ slightly but offer teachers the opportunity to share their thinking and ask questions and offer leaders ongoing opportunities to take the temperature of the staff, knowing where additional time and attention may be needed

Choice in professional development: Driven by explicit feedback from staff, leaders provide their teachers with meaningful choice in the ways that they grow professionally. From book studies, EdCamp-style learning, a selection of various workshops to choose from, and learning walks in other classrooms, we create space for agency in our learning communities by asking our learners what they are interested in knowing more about and how they'd like to get there. We provide space for teachers to make decisions about how they will use their workdays, showing them we trust them to design their own schedules to meet their learning styles and needs. Leaders know the needs of their teachers and are intentional with the time and focus they devote to professional learning.

Shared leadership: We want learners who are committed to our purpose and give them an active role as leaders. Teachers take on leadership roles as team or department heads and empower their voices as they help us make campus decisions and guide next steps we take together that align with our campus vision. We give them opportunities to learn and practice the skills they need as leaders, such as ways to move through difficult conversations with their colleagues, the art of listening and asking questions, and the roles necessary for true collaboration with one another.

How of curriculum: While our states and districts have mandated standards that help us vertically align and spiral learning experiences for students, we explicitly give teachers permission to pause to best determine how this learning will unfold in each of our classrooms. With this space, we give teachers a platform to use their voice—what they know about their students as learners

and their curriculum—in their unit maps and lesson designs. We further empower their agency by encouraging them to think critically about their curriculum and try new things to meet the interests and unique needs of their students. With intentional risk and reflection, teachers are responsive to the learning and then have the space needed to co-construct their curriculum with their students.

Curiosity

Those who lead with a lens of inquiry are keenly aware and take notice of the dispositions they embody in their roles. In Chapter 3, we outlined the dispositions of an inquiry leader, highlighting how this quality and mindset impacts the way we approach, listen, and lean in. As we continue to lead and embody these dispositions with more depth and complexity, we find ourselves flexing our thinking about the impact that our own curiosity has on our teachers, students, and schools. So what does it mean to show up as a curious leader? What does a curious leader say and do? And perhaps most importantly, how does our own curiosity help nurture a culture of inquiry in our school buildings?

It is imperative that our learners see us tinkering with ideas, leaning into the learning, and asking questions that are grounded in pure interest and wonder. Curious leaders take notice and observe and position themselves in and around their school buildings to be able to do so. We take this stance in the way that we connect and interact with the quality time we spend inside classrooms—the way we pull up a chair to sit with teachers who are collaboratively working with one another, how we eagerly kneel down to settle in deeper in the learning with students, and the way we warmly greet, engage, and connect with students at the door.

Reimagining our roles as leaders: As inquiry leaders, we rethink and reimagine the way we show up in our roles as leaders. *We get in the learning.* With a playful mindset, we reflect on the ways we leverage our positions in our schools and consider how to move more toward a constructivist approach to teaching and learning. By means of asking questions and the intentional time we spend in classrooms, we are able to co-design and facilitate professional learning opportunities with and for our learners. The direction we take with these sessions stems from the learners themselves. We lift up the inquiries we hear in team meetings and gather additional feedback and other formal and informal data points to co-construct meaningful learning experiences for our learners. We continue to rethink our roles by being mindful of how we engage with our learners. We attend team and department meetings with a mindset to learn rather than tell, co-construct rather than dictate. At these meetings, we refrain from speaking first, instead positioning ourselves to be part of the learning in a new way. We reconsider how we show up, staying open-minded and ever more curious about the impact this different mindset has on those we lead.

Notice, observe, and wonder: How does one build their capacity for curiosity? How do we tune in and find out more about ourselves, the impact of our leadership, and the students and teachers we serve? Inquiry leaders take stock of what they see. They dedicate time to notice and observe and use these experiences to provoke new thinking and ask more questions. If you were to look at my weekly calendar, you'd find several hours each week blocked off with "learning walks" in classrooms and walking the halls. These learning walks are just that—opportunities for me to frame my mindset as I step out of my office and into hallways and classrooms. Armed with only my phone to capture artifacts and other evidence of learning and growth as a campus, these are invaluable hours that give me space to put on a learning lens and notice what's unfolding in classrooms.

I vigorously listen to small group conversations of students working on a project, observe how each teacher uniquely facilitates student inquiries within their already-well-thought-out lessons, and, more often than not, will pull up a seat next to a student and ask them to share more about what they are learning. These brief conversations help me connect with the students in our building and give me a clear picture of the ways that they are experiencing the learning within the classrooms. I ask students to share their feelings about learning with me, what challenges they've recently come across with this particular topic, and, most importantly, what new wonderings or questions are emerging based on what they are exploring. Later, I'll circle back with the teacher and explain more about something I noticed in the conversation but lift it up as a question.

In my sharing, I'm intentional with how this interaction, even brief, stirred my curiosity and made me wonder more about the direction that the lesson would be taking next, how the teacher planned on making space for students to reflect on their learning to inform their next steps, or even what provocations were used to activate student thinking before I stepped foot into the classroom that day. We refine our skills to notice, observe, and question by making time and space for it. We take a closer look at our weekly schedules and reconsider how we use our time with our learners. If we step forward with the intention to lead with this lens, this can be done. With a constructivist approach to our roles, we continually stretch ourselves to embody the mindset of a learner, carefully balancing the role we play in leading with this lens while juggling the demands of our portfolios. We notice and observe, and we wonder and continually question to remind ourselves that there is always something else to uncover and something new to explore to cultivate the cultures of inquiry we are so deeply passionate about.

Celebrating the learning: In the educational landscape, we tend to celebrate our learners in traditional, expected, and formal ways. We hold up an accomplishment or celebration of a job well done at the start of a staff meeting or weekly internal newsletters, highlighting the person and reinforcing the culture and community we are trying to cultivate. And while these forms of celebration are essential in building and embracing relationships with our teachers, there's another way I find essential in celebrating the learning with my learners; it's called "The Go Back."

Nurturing a Culture of Inquiry

The Go Back is a mindful move I return to time and time again in my professional practice and consider a powerful way to elevate the process of learning. It shows teachers that I care and am curious about what's unfolding in the process of learning; it also builds their reflective capacities, providing me with a powerful structure to ask questions and model my own reflections and curiosities.

After I visit a classroom during my weekly learning walks and have shared a resource I found on Twitter with a teacher or recently facilitated a campus-wide professional learning session, I'm mindful about checking in and *going back* to my learners to reassess where their learning has taken them since we last interacted with one another. I'll start these conversations with language that models my own reflective thinking, such as, "I was doing some reflecting since our professional development session last week, and it made me wonder . . ." or "I'm curious to know some of your thoughts about the resource I sent your way. It made me think about you, and I'm curious to know what questions came up for you when you saw it," or even "I noticed that during our learning walk last week you expressed some interesting ideas but were still mulling them over. How's that going for you? Where has your thinking taken you since then?" The Go Back shows our learners we value the *process of learning*—not solely the end result of what happens when we get there—and celebrate all that unfolds within this process.

Reflection

Inquiry educators talk not only about what they are doing with their students but also about how they are getting there with them. They take careful notes about the things they notice and listen to what and how their learners are responding to the learning in the classrooms. They mindfully plan for provocations and use the framework of the inquiry cycle to structure the learning experiences they plan for. As

I've outlined in several chapters within this book, reflection continually lies at the heart of our inquiry practice and leverages the work we do with our students.

Feedback is a form of reflection we use as inquiry leaders. We are mindful and intentional with how and when we ask for and use feedback from our learners. Feedback helps us steer the collective vision of our campus, builds trusting relationships with our learners who feel safe enough to share their thinking, and models our value of focusing on the whole teacher. As we continue to nurture and cultivate a culture of inquiry, we are attentive to the structures that help us gather feedback about what is really happening with our learners, not what we think is happening or who the loudest voices in the room are. Cue the power of the Post-it.

In Chapter 6, I've shared with you the ways we make learning visible for our learners. In my office, you'll find an ever-changing learning wall full of artifacts that illustrate the work we are doing together as a campus. The wall includes photos, our campus vision statement, and dozens and dozens of Post-its. These three-by-three squares are invaluable to me as an inquiry leader. They include the thinking and questions of my learners and give me the feedback I need to determine our next steps as a learning community. While invaluable to me, these small pieces of paper are merely another scrap if not structured in a way that gives an equitable voice to all learners. As we continue to facilitate reflection through the inquiry framework, we remain intentional with how we scaffold and support our learners' reflective thinking. While there are endless ways you can structure reflection, below are several I rely on heavily. Their simple yet powerful nature provides me with the feedback I need as a leader, but they also are easily translated to the classroom. As I peak into classrooms, I quite often see evidence of teachers taking the structures we are using together in our professional learning with their students.

This is just another reminder that what we do with our adult learners impacts the approaches to teaching and learning in the classrooms. The more we embody and model the dispositions of an inquiry leader, the more our learners take on these dispositions as their own.

Question Sort: Sorting allows our learners to make connections to their thinking, further explore ideas, and begin to make sense of their thinking. It's a vital process of the inquiry cycle and gives our learners opportunities to organize ideas and build the skill of reflection. After a professional learning session with teams of teachers, I'll call on them to reflect on their thinking in the form of questions, using the prompt: *What new wonderings or questions do you have?*

After we've generated the questions, I post them in a collective space where all of the Post-its are visible (at this time, there is no order to where they post their questions). Then I prompt the group to pause and observe the collection of questions. This quiet noticing of all questions acts as the scaffolded thinking for the next step in the sort. I then call on teachers to begin to group questions in the way they best see fit. You may notice a grouping of questions by topic, concept, or perhaps by question type (skinny vs. thick). At this stage, it's important that we don't critique, judge, or analyze the questions but rather leverage the sorting that has occurred to guide next steps.

Following this sorting activity, I'll return to my office or meet with other campus leaders and take note of the ways the questions were grouped. We'll look for question trends and the ways that our learners grouped and sorted their thinking and jot down questions *we have* about their questions. We'll also revisit our campus goals and professional learning plans and timelines, making adjustments as needed to fit the ways our learners' feedback helps us shape the direction of learning. These question sorts frame and support the reflective thinking of *all learners*.

GOGO & WMYST: We keep in mind that the less talking we do, the more our learners have space to do so themselves, taking true ownership over their learning. Yet too often, I observe teachers casually prompting their students to turn and talk to a partner after a big concept is presented. And while this focused time to discuss their thinking with their peers is well intended, it's a missed opportunity for more mindfulness and intention with this learning structure. In order to scaffold and nudge our learners' thinking and conversations in the direction we masterfully know they need to go, we must facilitate and use structures to get them there. A simple sentence structure or other scaffolded frame leverages the time that we devote to these collaborative conversations.

While we plan for and design professional learning sessions with our teachers, we consider our intentional use of these talk structures to nudge our learners to do more of the heavy lifting in the learning. Give One, Get One (GOGO) is a great frame to support our learners to reflect and share more of their thinking with colleagues. I use this routine to guide breakout conversations yet add another talk structure, What Makes You Say That? (WMYST), to further engage learners in a reflective mindset.

As teachers pair up with one another to share their thinking and gather new ideas from their colleagues, as the GOGO recommends, I ask the listener to respond to their partner with this question. This does two important things in learning. The speaker in the group is encouraged to further reflect and dig deeper into their thinking and ideas while the listener practices the vital skill of listening at a new level. The listener isn't just waiting for their chance to speak, to give their rebuttal, or to agree mindlessly. The listener *actually listens*. The roles are then reversed, and yet another opportunity for intentional sharing, reflection, and listening unfolds.

Compass Points: We've adopted yet another thinking routine from the work of Ron Ritchhart and Mark Church, called Compass Points (you've already seen evidence of this routine in a previous chapter).[8] This reflective structure supports our learners to think about their

Nurturing a Culture of Inquiry

thinking and gives us multiple perspectives to explore later and use to inform our next steps.

I routinely use Compass Points the way Ritchhart and Church have outlined in the book, but I also love the flexibility that this thinking routine provides. By simply changing some of the language on each of the points to meet the type of feedback I am seeking from my learners, I encourage and promote the culture that we are continually working at moving toward. I playfully change out the points on each end of the compass, using words and phrases such as *noticing* or *next steps, explore next* or *enlightened thinking, wonderings* or *supports needed to move forward in learning*. Not all of the points need to be revised when using this routine, of course, but I always consider what I need as a leader to facilitate our next steps and how my learners have synthesized their learning based on our experiences with one another.

Collaborative Learning

A huge underpinning of an inquiry educator is the co-constructing of learning with our learners. Another way we continue to model this unique quality of inquiry learning is by leveling out the playing field to further co-construct the learning with one another. We may never be able to fully step outside our roles as evaluators, but we begin to reframe the ways teachers view our roles within their learning. We eliminate assumptions by being transparent about our "why," build trust with our staff by showing genuine interest and commitment to their professional growth, and experience our leadership with tenderness toward the reflective nature of inquiry learning.

There are two powerful approaches we take to collaborative learning as we harness this approach and sit further in the learning with our learners, moving away from compliance and complacency toward social constructivism, giving our teachers and ourselves *time to learn*.

New teacher cohort: As we invite new staff into our learning communities, we evaluate the structures we have in place for welcoming them and consider the influence to further the culture of inquiry we are so mindful of cultivating. In Chapter 4, we introduced you to the system we have in place to support staff who were joining our campus. Early on, we introduce and use the inquiry cycle to frame our time with our new learners, establishing a clear constructivist practice. Keeping the end in mind, we consider our campus vision and feedback from the previous year's cohort and curate a list of topics for us to explore with one another. As I build our agendas, I always ensure I've carved out space for reflection and feedback from my learners, am mindful of not overplanning, and remain open-minded and flexible to the interests and needs of my new staff.

Together, we engage in learning walks both on and off campus; we play and have fun with our staff by tinkering with new ideas, digging deep into questions provoked by book studies, an insightful article, or a series of videos. I am transparent in the purpose of this cohort and allow the new staff to shape and direct the learning while softly anchoring myself in our vision as an inquiry leader. If you haven't already, go ahead and revisit Chapter 4. What new connections can you make about the impact of this structure? How can you leverage the time you spend with your new staff to reinforce your connected values of inquiry and its collaborative approach to learning?

Learning walks: How do we make learning personal, meaningful, and authentic? We ask our learners about the things that they are curious about and the areas they identify they want to explore in their practice further. We rethink our mandated goal-setting systems and encourage our staff to actively engage in personal inquiries that empower their practice and become agents of their own learning. From campus leaders to classroom teachers, I am a huge advocate for inquiry educators to get into classrooms. Learning walks help us see firsthand what amazing practices and approaches to learning are occurring right within the four walls of our building.

Opening up our classroom doors and welcoming one another into our learning spaces connects us as a collaborative learning community, further engaging us within a culture of inquiry. As with all learning experiences, inquiry leaders are intentional and purposeful with these learning walks. The structuring of these experiences stems from individual teacher or grade-level goals, questions that bubble up from a previous campus-based professional learning session, or simply giving our learners the space and freedom to explore and have fun with their own learning. We frame and provoke the thinking prior to these learning walks by checking in with our learners, lifting up their questions, and nudging our learners to pause. Learners gather evidence with a sense of wonder, and we harness the power of the "Go Back" to support them in reflecting and making connections to their personal inquiries. We stretch their thinking with questions and challenge them to listen and look with inquisitiveness and heightened curiosity about what they might uncover.

Hiring Practices
Who Helps You Cultivate Your Garden?

We lead, embody, and value an inquiry mindset. We cultivate safe spaces for our teachers to be playful and take risks. We ask our teachers to reconsider their approach to their practice, moving away from teaching and learning that values the "right" answer to one that considers the whole child and provides meaningful and relevant learning experiences. And yet, how does our approach to hiring and bringing in new staff model these similar values? How often do many of us find ourselves in conference rooms or sitting across from candidates with the same set of questions we've used from year to year, almost already knowing what we'll hear from the other side of the table?

At the start of this chapter, we introduced the concept of a garden and how the foundational layer of soil ensures that these green spaces flourish. Like soil, who you bring into your organization and your team is important. We again ask ourselves in what ways this garden, like inquiry, can flourish. What values do we nurture to cultivate the conditions for rich and meaningful learning for both teachers and our students?

Who will help you cultivate this garden?

While many of us have different contexts or expectations in hiring new staff, we still ask ourselves how our approach to hiring can be different, how bringing on new staff helps us cultivate a culture of inquiry, and how we consider new ways to co-construct *with our learners*. What if instead of the "dog and pony show," we undid the system we were a part of, approaching the time we spend bringing in new staff a bit more mindfully, a bit more curiously, and a bit more playfully?

In Chapter 4, we asked you to take an inventory of your own values. Now it's time to take stock of what values are represented in your campus vision statement, what you and your staff value in one another as a collaborative learning community, and what value a new perspective could bring. Below are several examples of values that may align with what's needed to grow as a school of inquiry. Bring these to your staff, have them generate some of their own, jot down their thinking, ask questions of one another, and engage in a reflective conversation to co-construct a list of your own values. To get the conversation started, you may even consider asking your staff to engage and assess their own values.

Values

- Creativity
- Innovative and continually searching for ways to bring best practices to students
- Open-minded
- Reflective

- Balance and personal wellness
- Playful
- Curiosity
- Communicator
- Growth mindset
- Not afraid of failure
- Going slow and not rushing the process
- Listening to all staff when there is discourse

Now that you have a list of values, it's time to get playful! One way to get playful in this process is by asking questions. I introduced you to a questioning protocol called the Question Formulation Technique (QFT), mentioned previously in this book. I'm a big fan of structures like these that nurture teacher agency and ensure an equitable voice for all learners. If you have not engaged in this questioning routine with your learners, now is a great time to get started. The questions I've included below have been generated with the Question Formulation Technique and reflect some of the values within this section. Perhaps you will consider adding some of these after your staff has generated their own as a provocation to kickstart your brainstorming session, or you will share some of them in the middle of the protocol when you notice your learners' questioning stalling.

Questions

- What have you created lately?
- How do you know when a child is not progressing?
- Name something you have intentionally stopped doing in your teaching practice.
- How would the student you consider the most difficult describe you?
- How do you feel about ambiguity?
- Describe a time you failed that led you to be a better colleague or teacher.

- If your classroom had a hashtag, what would it be and why?
- How do you inspire your students to take action?
- Describe something you've done that's innovative.
- What on your resume are you most proud of and why?
- During PLC (Professional Learning Community), you want to share a new idea with your team. How would you share your idea with your team to get their buy-in? What materials or resources would you bring to your team? Consider the interview panel as your teammates.

Need a few more questions to bring to your staff before the interview process? Are you curious to see what other innovative thinkers are asking during the hiring process? Check out this thread on Twitter to collect some additional questions or tweak some of the ones you and your colleagues have already generated.

We continue to tend to our gardens, mindful of the organic way they grow and flourish under our watchful eyes. Inquiry leaders start small yet play the "long game," knowing that each of the moves we make, questions we ask, and structures we redefine will nurture a culture that allows inquiry to thrive for all learners.

* What does your campus already value that nurtures a culture of inquiry? What actions do you take as an inquiry leader that nurture these values?
* Which of the practices presented in this chapter do you think could have the biggest impact on student learning? On teacher agency?
* Revisit the questions you use when bringing people into your team. How do they reflect your values? What do they bring that cultivates an environment that allows space for inquiry to flourish?

A Call to Action

At the start of this book, I shared the questions that provoked new ideas and thinking about leadership. You have read stories about the impact an inquiry mindset had on teachers, the critical friends and thought partners who remained committed to the process, reflecting and open to reimagining the traditional roles of leadership. They considered how leading with a lens of inquiry brought transformation toward a school culture that honors the learner in ways some of our current systems will never be able to do.

Our exploration and learning about our roles as inquiry leaders is never quite over. There will always be an area to refine, a new perspective to explore, and more questions that emerge. And while some may consider this an exhaustive process, an inquiry leader understands this is the reason we lead with this lens. The questions, experiences with learners, and reflections along the way help shape who we are.

Revisit the intention you set for yourself in the introduction of this book.

Revisit the questions I've posed throughout the chapters.

Revisit your reflections, the notes you've made in the margins, the pages you've tabbed, and the sections you've highlighted.

Now, notice how they've changed over the course of your reading.

How have your reflections, your questions, your notes shaped your growth toward *leading with an inquiry mindset*?

As I conclude, I'll present you with one final call to action. We further embody the mindset of an inquiry leader when we are actively engaged in an inquiry process with our learners. Using the inquiry framework I presented in Chapter 1, I have summarized actionable steps inquiry leaders take on a daily basis *and* the ways that they continually reflect during this process. I leave you with more questions than we started this journey with. Perhaps the action steps and reflection prompts will give you more of the language you were searching for; perhaps they become a roadmap to ground you through the ambiguous nature of inquiry, or perhaps these become a provocation to be explored with other leaders you engage with.

Your use of this final resource is the culmination of your learning throughout the book. It's worth revisiting the image of the inquiry cycle in Chapter 1. Reflection, said many times throughout this book, remains at the heart of inquiry. There is no checklist or exact set of steps to engage in the inquiry process. The reflective questions are there to help center the process *around* continuous learning. Using this resource *powerfully* and *intentionally* will rely on you bringing all of your learning from your reading to this framework. Let's take a look now:

Leading through the Inquiry Process

Tuning In	
Actions Inquiry Leaders Take	Reflection as the Leader
• In classrooms, listening to teaching and learning • Attends team meetings, engages in whole-body listening • Models curiosity, participates in the PD as a learner • Gets into the halls and talks with students • Adds equitable talk frameworks when planning agenda items for meetings	• How can what I see/notice/hear inform my next steps? • What am I hearing? What am I not hearing? • What are the students doing? Saying? • What am I curious to know more about? • How will I make this thinking visible and transparent to teachers? • How are my actions and ways of showing up building relationships with the teachers? • What stage am I in as a "part" of the team? What's my role? • What questions can I ask to help take the learning further? • What questions can I ask to help nudge the learning and the learner?

Finding Out	
Actions Inquiry Leaders Take	Reflection as the Leader
• Actively listens during team meetings • Searches for additional resources to support learner interests and questions. Uses PLN to gather additional perspectives • Asks questions during team meetings and one-on-one with teachers, connecting to larger school vision, as well as teacher-specific questions related to goals, strengths, etc. • Engages in learning walks (classrooms, other campuses, other community resources) • Asks for reflections and other forms of feedback, including weekly check-in forms, informal check-ins and hallway conversations, etc.	• What types of questions are my teachers asking? • What does this data tell me? • What am I learning about the teachers' thinking? • What are the tasks, frameworks, or experiences that I (or my teachers) are engaged in that allow us to gather evidence? • What is the evidence? • How will I gather the evidence? • How do I make this evidencing visible and transparent to teachers?

Sorting

Actions Inquiry Leaders Take	Reflection as the Leader
• Collaborates between campus leaders • Collaborates with classroom teachers • Models the desired thinking, questioning environment, and reflective thinking • Revisits gathered resources and other professional resources and sorts them in useful ways, using tools such as digital folders, Padlet, Pocket, etc. • Revisits the learning wall for both teacher and campus, making sense of the evidence, organizing it, and looking for trends, patterns, themes, etc. • Asks learners what they are noticing based on the evidence gathered during learning walks, professional learning sessions, the conclusion of lessons, or items discussed during a team meeting	• What do I notice? What do I wonder? What do I know? • Where might we go next together? • What questions can I ask to help take the learning further? • What questions can I ask to help nudge the learning and the learner? • What additional ways can I support the learning? • How can we recognize our biases and flatten the process for all to engage? • How can we minimize complacency and maximize equity for teachers to engage in this process? • What other perspectives am I not including? How am I leaving space for other perspectives?

Going Further	
Actions Inquiry Leaders Take	Reflection as the Leader
• Professional development and resources tailored to team and teacher needs • Consistently nudges and shares resources via PLN to continue informal PD • Grows personal PLN, taking the opportunity to gain new perspectives, ways to connect with teachers, etc. • Uses evidence to guide next steps • Shows how teachers' voice and engagement (i.e., evidence) was used to shape next steps and make them transparent • Uses the "Go Back" method with learners, nudging their thinking with open-ended questions • Asks more questions and takes notice of how the evidence is similar or different throughout the earlier experiences with learners	• Have I gathered enough evidence? How do I know? • What challenges or roadblocks are emerging in learning? How might I find out more about their root cause? • What questions can I ask to help take the learning further? • What questions can I ask to help nudge the learning and the learner? • How am I intentionally connecting my learner questions and interests to our work with one another? • Where else might I explore?

Drawing Conclusions	
Actions Inquiry Leaders Take	Reflection as the Leader
• Actively engages with teachers in reflection; gathers evidence using teacher reflections and feedback • Makes personal reflections in inquiry journal • Connects actions to campus vision and mission, teacher and campus goals, etc. • Revisits the questions, the evidence, and the connections made throughout the process; invites learners to take notice of the learning that has occurred	• How have we been purposeful in answering questions from learners? • What do I now understand about my learners? The learning? • How will I gather feedback from my learners about how they feel about their learning? • How do I feel about our learning? • I used to think . . . Now I wonder . . . • What is the new evidence telling me about our next steps? • How do I celebrate and share the learning that's unfolded?
Taking Action	
Actions Inquiry Leaders Take	Reflection as the Leader
• Shares resources related to planning and creates materials/resources for teachers, etc., in team meetings • Celebrates successes, small wins, areas of growth, etc. • Provides additional support and professional learning opportunities • Creates and modifies campus action plans • Brings learning and shares the process of learning with stakeholders and the community	• I used to think . . . Now I know . . . • What questions can I ask to help us summarize the learning? • How will our learning shape the learning experience for others? • How could we have improved the process? What would we have done differently? • How can we take this learning deeper or continue to have it inform our practice, our school, and our community?

Now is the time to take your learning in a way that is uniquely yours. After reading *Leading with a Lens of Inquiry,* you will need the support of other leaders and inquiry educators, feedback from your learners, and a mindset that remains curious and playful. Document your journey, ask more questions, gather the artifacts and evidence, and add your voice to the collective #leadingwithinquiry community.

Do it for yourself.

Do it for those you lead.

Do it for the students who ultimately benefit from leaders like you who had the courage to rethink the systems that have stifled creativity—ones that have valued performance over the natural process of learning and systems that have forgotten about the whole child and the whole teacher.

I'll set you on your journey the same way we got you started—with a question and nudge to invite you to step forward and be the inquiry leader you've always had within you.

You are ready.

Now, let's get started, shall we?

Suggested Reading

As explored in chapter two, inquiry leaders extend an invitation to try new things. The collection of reading here is just that, an invitation. Which of these titles already live on your bookshelf, heavily marked and tabbed and fondly lent out to your colleagues? Which of these are new or unfamiliar to you? I encourage you to add a few to your collection of resources as you continue to build your knowledge about the school of thinking that supports leading with a lens of inquiry. As you connect with these titles, I hope they support your continuing journey in the way that they have supported mine. We don't become inquiry leaders by happenstance. With critical friends, reflection, and further learning, we continue to explore a body of work that's been decades in the making.

Aguilar, Elena. *The Art of Coaching*. Hoboken, NJ: Jossey Bass, 2013.

Aguilar, Elena. *The Art of Coaching Teams*. Hoboken, NJ: John Wiley & Sons, 2016.

Berger, Warren. *A More Beautiful Question: The Power of Inquiry to Spark Breakthrough Ideas*. London, UK: Bloomsbury Publishing, 2014.

Berger, Warren. *The Book of Beautiful Questions*. London, UK: Bloomsbury Publishing, 2019.

Claxton, Guy, Robert Cleary, Gemma Goldenberg, Rachel Macfarlane, Graham Powell, and Jann Robinson. *Powering Up Your School: The Learning Power Approach to School Leadership.* United Kingdom: Crown House Publishing, 2017.

Costa, Arthur L. and Bena Kallic. *Habits of Mind Across the Curriculum: Practical and Creative Strategies for Teachers.* Alexandria, VA: ASCD, 2009.

Dearybury, Jed and Julie P. Jones. *The Playful Classroom: The Power of Play for All Ages.* Hoboken, NJ: Jossey-Bass, 2020.

Halbert, Judy and Linda Kaser. *Leading through Spirals of Inquiry: For Equity and Quality.* Winnipeg, Manitoba: Portage and Main Press, 2022.

MacKenzie, Trevor and Rebecca Bathurst-Hunt. *Inquiry Mindset: Nurturing the Dreams, Wonders, and Curiosities of Our Youngest Learners.* Del Mar, CA: Elevate Books Edu, 2019.

Mitchell, Kimberly L. *Experience Inquiry: 5 Powerful Strategies, 50 Practical Experiences.* Thousand Oaks, CA: Corwin, 2018.

Murdoch, Kath. *The Power of Inquiry: Teaching and Learning with Curiosity, Creativity, and Purpose in the Contemporary Classroom.* Seastar Education, 2015.

Nottingham, James A. *The Learning Challenge: How to Guide Your Students through the Learning Pit to Achieve Deeper Understanding.* Thousand Oaks, CA: Corwin, 2017.

Ritchhart, Ron, Mark Church, and Karin Morrison. *Making Thinking Visible: How to Promote Engagement, Understanding, and Independence for All Learners.* Hoboken, NJ: Jossey Bass Wiley, 2011.

Robinson, Sir Ken and Lou Aronica. *Creative Schools: The Grassroots Revolution That's Transforming Education.* New York: Penguin Books, 2016.

Rothstein, Dan and Luz Santana. *Make Just One Change: Teach Students to Ask Their Own Questions.* Cambridge, MA: Harvard Education Press, 2011.

Wheatley, Margaret J. *Turning to One Another: Simple Conversations to Restore Hope to the Future.* Oakland, CA: Berrett-Koehler Publishers, 2009.

Wiggins, Grant and Jay McTighe. *Understanding by Design*, 2nd edition. London: Pearson, 2005.

Bibliography

Foreword

1. Ginott, Haim G. *Teacher and Child: A Book for Parents and Teachers.* New York: Avon, 1972.
2. Kaser, Linda, and Judy Halbert. *Leadership Mindsets: Innovation and Learning in the Transformation of Schools (Leading School Transformation Book 4).* London: Routledge, 2009.
3. Lieberman, A., and L. Miller. (2005) "Teachers as Leaders." *The Educational Forum* 69, no. 2 (2005): 151-162.
4. Riordan, R., and S. Caillier. *Schools as Equitable Communities of Inquiry.* Riordan, Palgrave Macmillan, 2018.

Chapter 1

1. Murdoch, Kath. *The Power of Inquiry: Teaching and Learning with Curiosity, Creativity, and Purpose in the Contemporary Classroom.* Seastar Education, 2015.

Chapter 2

2. Ritchhart, Ron, Mark Church, and Karin Morrison. *Making Thinking Visible: How to Promote Engagement, Understanding, and Independence for All Learners.* Hoboken, NJ: Jossey Bass Wiley, 2011.

Chapter 3

3. MacKenzie, Trevor and Rebecca Bathurst-Hunt. *Inquiry Mindset: Nurturing the Dreams, Wonders, and Curiosities of our Youngest Learners.* Del Mar, CA: Elevate Books Edu, 2019.

Chapter 5

4. Ritchhart, Ron, Mark Church, and Karin Morrison. *Making Thinking Visible: How to Promote Engagement, Understanding, and Independence for All Learners.* Hoboken, NJ: Jossey Bass Wiley, 2011.
5. Rothstein, Dan and Luz Santana. *Make Just One Change: Teach Students to Ask Their Own Questions.* Cambridge, MA: Harvard Education Press, 2011.
6. Nottingham, James. "James Nottingham's Learning Challenge (Learning Pit) Animation." *YouTube* video, 11:30. November 23, 2013. https://youtu.be/3IMUAOhuO78.
7. Aguilar, Elena. *The Art of Coaching.* Hoboken, NJ: Jossey Bass, 2013.

Chapter 7

8. Ritchhart, Ron, Mark Church, and Karin Morrison. *Making Thinking Visible: How to Promote Engagement, Understanding, and Independence for All Learners.* Hoboken, NJ: Jossey Bass Wiley, 2011.

Acknowledgments

I have to start by thanking my husband, Jake. From taking our boys out for weekend adventures so I could have quiet space to focus and write, to your enthusiasm and questions about a body of work that's quite unlike your professional one, you were an essential part of getting this book completed. I'm so very grateful for your love and support for a project you know I'm so very passionate about. I love you, babe!

To my colleague and dear friend, Julie Haney, for nudging me toward the book you have in your hands. The big questions we asked of one another, the out-of-the-box thinking we explored, and genuine loving support for the work—even when it didn't unfold in the way we had expected—are all greatly appreciated. Thank you, Julie, for helping me grow as a leader and planting seeds for something that's become even bigger than I could have imagined on my own.

I continue to be inspired and shaped as an educator by my friend and principal, Doriane Marvel. Your boundless joy and inspiring leadership are grounded in an authenticity not found in many. Your commitment to learning, reflection, and innovation—all the while honoring the voices of your learners, including mine—are evident in each of your interactions and steps as a leader. I was fortunate enough to have written this book while in your leadership, and your support throughout this year has given me the confidence to do so. I continue to look to you for inspiration, and I hope you see your values interwoven into who I have become.

Nathan Wisdom, your guidance, both on and off my yoga mat, has given me the tools for a more mindful approach to daily life musings and has grounded me in the best of ways. I've learned how to listen in the way that's necessary to experience life fully. The way I show up for myself and others is the result of your teachings. Namaste.

I must of course mention my critical friends and thought partners whom I've called on well before even writing this book. My hope is that all of you see yourselves in the stories I've shared and within the reflections and questions I've left for each of the readers. The phone calls to sort through thinking and big ideas, the countless cups of cappuccino at the coffee shop down the street from my house, and all the conversations in between have helped to shape the ideas presented here. I value your expertise and appreciate your attention to a project you know represents my passion. I'm ever inspired by your words, support, and of course, questions that challenge my thinking and keep me curious. Thank you. Endlessly.

And a very special thank you to the leaders and big thinkers who've come before me and continue to inspire and stretch me to this day. Countless to name and a list that's ever growing (Where would I be without the stacks of books by my side?), the work of Sir Ken Robinson, Kath Murdoch, Elena Aguilar, Grant Wiggins, Ron Ritchhart, Tony Wagner, Michael Stone, Brené Brown, and Margaret Wheatley are just a few I'll leave here today. Your voices are the reason my work lives here today. I'm humbled and inspired by your great minds!

About the Author

With a professional teaching and leadership background in both private and public international schools (IB PYP Educator & PYP Coordinator), Jessica Vance brings a unique perspective to her role as Enrichment & Environment Coordinator. Her passion for student centered learning, collaboration, and coaching stems from the students themselves, finding inspiration in their natural curiosity as they authentically engage in learning experiences inside and outside of the classroom. Jessica strongly believes in the power of leading with a lens of inquiry, facilitating innovative professional learning opportunities and coaching sessions that provide the space for educators to collaborate and reflect, while supporting their professional growth as inquiry practitioners.

Her journey and experience as an inquiry educator in IB schools and Place Based Education fuels her passion and global work in coaching both teachers and leaders in their roles, as well as supporting schools in implementing inquiry-based learning. Jessica understands the power of curiosity to guide next steps, creating the space we all need as learners as we actively engage in a reflective practice. In her published book, *Leading with a Lens of Inquiry*, she outlines the ways in which we, as leaders, need to support and facilitate our teachers in the same ways in which we want our teachers to engage with their students.

Twitter & Instagram @jess_vanceedu
Website leadingwithinquiry.com

About the Illustrator

Ryan Bear is a visual storyteller currently based in Portland, Oregon. With a background in animation and digital media arts, his focus is in illustration and motion art. He's been a part of many projects ranging from personalized family commissions, whimsical children's books, thoughtful commercial work, zippy animations to preproduction in storyboards and character design.

Through his mastery of technique and vivid imagination, he prides himself on delivering quality work. Every piece has an intentional balance of craft and his clients' authenticity. With a big emphasis on the creative process, he dives deep with clients to bring their vision into fruition. He is known for being immaculate and putting in the extra mile for the project to reach its full potential.

Instagram @ryanbearart

Website ryanbearart.com